THE COMPLETE
MICROWAVE
COOKBOOK

TIGER BOOKS INTERNATIONAL
LONDON

A QUINTET BOOK

This edition first published 1988 by
Tiger Books International Ltd.
London.
Copyright © 1988 Quintet Publishing Limited
ISBN 1 870461 64 9

This book was designed and produced by
Quintet Publishing Limited
6 Blundell Street
London N7 9BH

Design Director: Peter Bridgewater
Art Director: Ian Hunt
Designer: Stuart Walden
Contributing Authors: Valerie Barrett,
Veronica Bull, Elizabeth Cornish,
Elaine Hallgarten, Bernice Hurst, Linda Sonntag
and Myra Street
Editors: Bridget Jones, Belinda Giles

Typeset in Great Britain by
Central Southern Typesetters, Eastbourne
Manufactured in Hong Kong by
Regent Publishing Services Limited
Printed in Hong Kong by Leefung-Asco
Printers Ltd.

This book contains material used in previous
publications.

Contents

Introduction

For years the art of food preparation and cooking has remained the same, based on well-tried methods and scientific facts that ensure success with even the most delicate mixtures. The microwave cooker offers a totally new form of energy for cooking food – red hot grills and firey ovens have been replaced by an invisible source of heat. With this new method of cooking comes a whole new set of rules that must be applied whenever anything is cooked by microwaves.

MICROWAVE ENERGY

There are just one or two basic facts about the way in which microwave energy cooks food that can be helpful when deciding on the best method of preparing dishes in the microwave. Microwaves are produced in a component known as a magnetron and are fed into the oven where they are distributed, usually by means of a wave stirrer. Even wave distribution is the key to even cooking; in addition most ovens have a turntable to move food through the microwaves as they circulate in the oven cavity. If an oven does not have a turntable it does not mean that it will cook unevenly – many of the ovens without turntables give excellent results with the advantage of providing cooking space for large square and oblong dishes.

Microwaves respond to different materials in different ways. They are reflected off metals in the same way as light waves are reflected off mirrors. They pass through glassware and a variety of other materials that are commonly used for cooking – china, some plastics and, to a certain extent, earthenware. The microwaves are absorbed by other substances – food substances in particular.

Once in the oven, the waves are reflected off the walls to hit the food. The microwaves then penetrate the food and are absorbed by it. The depth of penetration depends on the type of food but an average maximum depth is 5 cm/2 in. The microwaves have the effect of vibrating certain minute particles – the water molecules – within the food. All foods contain water, some more than others; and it is this moisture that produces the heat for cooking. The waves cause friction between the molecules so that heat is produced – just like the heat that results when two sticks are rubbed together. The heat generated within the food cooks the raw ingredients. Because the moisture content of the food is a key factor, the cooking method is moist and the ingredients give up a lot of their moisture in the form of steam. This is why the cooked results are often comparable with those obtained by steaming. The cooking time depends on the type of food – very dense, dry food takes a long time to cook. Food which is light cooks quickly. If there is a lot of liquid in the dish, it takes a long time to heat because there are so many water particles to be activated. For this reason, when a recipe requires a significant quantity of water or stock, boiling liquid is used – your kettle is your microwave's best friend!

COOKING CONTAINERS

METAL Metal containers **should not** be used in the microwave oven – they reflect the energy so the microwaves will not pass through to cook the food. Reflected microwaves can also cause damage to the magnetron, the main component of the oven. To complicate and confuse, small amounts of metal can be used in the microwave cooker under certain circumstances. If you have a large portion of food – for example a chicken – it will absorb most of the microwaves in the oven cavity. The bone-ends and sharp joints are prone to over-cooking, so they can be covered by small pieces of cooking foil. This small amount of foil will not cause any problems, in relation to the whole area of food, and will prevent the microwaves over-cooking the small area which it protects. You will also notice that certain foil containers for convenience foods can be put in the microwave cooker – these are usually very shallow and the foil surface is usually covered with food so that there is the minimum of reflection. The key to safety is to read – and follow – the manufacturer's instructions which will outline exactly the rules that apply to your oven.

HEATPROOF GLASSWARE This is ideal for use in the microwave. Brands such as Pyrex and Arcopal provide a wide variety of different shapes and sizes of cooking containers. Flan dishes are useful for cooking small items, allowing room for them to be set apart for even cooking. Jugs are useful for heating milk and making sauces – look out for 1.15 L/2 pt jugs which allow plenty of room for whisking during cooking. Cake dishes and loaf dishes (useful for meatloaves) are also available.

CHINA AND PORCELAIN Most plain heatproof china and ovenproof crockery can be used for cooking in the microwave. Avoid any items which have metal trims or metal paints used in the decoration. Mugs can be used for heating drinks or for melting small amounts of butter. Small dishes and basins are ideal for scrambling eggs or cooking small portions of foods like frozen peas.

EARTHENWARE Most earthenware can be used in the microwave. This does absorb a certain amount of the microwave energy and will become hot during cooking (even for short periods if it absorbs a significant amount of energy) – in some cases, the cooking time may be lengthened. Avoid very shiny metalic glazes as these have the same effect as metal and will cause sparking in the oven.

PLASTICS Some plastic containers can be used for defrosting and for warming food but unless they are designed for use in the microwave cooker, most plastic containers will soften if used for cooking or reheating food.

WOOD, BASKETS AND GLASSWARE All these can be used for briefly heating foods – warming bread rolls for example or warming a glass of milk – but they **should not** be put in the microwave for any length of time. Lead crystal **should not** be put in the microwave as it will cause sparking.

SPECIALIST MICROWAVE COOKWARE There is an enormous range of specialist cookware available. You will find that much of the material is plastic which is resistant to high temperatures and particularly well suited for the microwaves to pass through resulting in the quickest possible cooking time. If you already have a good supply of oven-proof glassware, ordinary mixing bowls and casserole dishes, think before you rush out and spend a small fortune on lots of specialist cookware that you are unlikely to use. Once you have had your microwave for a while you will soon discover which special dishes are ideal for your needs.

BROWNING DISHES These are designed to brown food that is cooked in the microwave oven – for example, chops, burgers and pizza bases. The base of the dish is coated with a substance which absorbs microwave energy in the same way as the food does. The dish is placed in the oven, empty, and the microwave energy is turned on for a prescribed length of time. At the end of this cooking period the base of the dish will be very hot – hot enough to sear meat or to brown a bread base for a pizza. The base does not retain the heat for a great length of time, so the first side browns lightly but it is difficult to brown the second side of the food if there are more than one or two items in the dish. The dishes are expensive – if you intend cooking lots of chops and burgers you will find a browning dish useful, otherwise think carefully before you part with your cash.

POWER SETTINGS

The first thing that you must do is to read your manufacturer's instruction book – it will provide all the back-up information that is essential before you begin to cook in your own oven. You must know at what power level your oven operates. The recipes in this book are tested for 650- and 700-watt ovens – if your oven operates at a lower power level, you will have to increase cooking times slightly; if it operates at a higher power level, you will find that cooking times are shorter than those suggested. If your oven is rated at 650 watts, then you will probably need the longest suggested cooking time but it is always advisable to start with the shortest time – you can do no harm by checking a dish in advance. Unlike conventional cooking, when you open the microwave door you will not ruin the food if it is uncooked – simply carry on cooking and watch cakes rise for a

second time!

Throughout the chapters, the power settings used are highlighted at the top of each recipe. The settings used refer to the following percentages of power:

> Full – 100 per cent
> Medium-high – 70 per cent
> Medium – 50 per cent
> Medium-low – 30 per cent
> Low – 10 per cent

Your microwave cooker may offer different terms for the power settings so follow the above guidelines to determine exactly how they relate to those used in the recipes.

GENERAL ADVICE ON MICROWAVE COOKING

The first thing is to be bold with your microwave – do not be afraid of it – and be ready to experiment but apply a little forethought beforehand. When you are cooking look in through the door to see what is happening – if something looks as though it is going drastically wrong, switch the oven off and remove the dish to see what has to be done. The following notes may be helpful if you are new to microwave cookers – as you get to know your oven you will develop your own set of hints and do's and don'ts as with any other cooking method.

CONTAINER SIZE If you are cooking a significant quantity of ingredients, or foods that are likely to boil over, use a big container – a mixing bowl is often ideal. For example, risottos, dishes of mixed vegetables and poultry or casserole-type dishes all benefit from being cooked in a large dish, allowing plenty of room for boiling up and stirring.

LIQUID CONTENT There is no strict rule for the quantities of liquid to use – when cooking vegetables you should not add lots of water. Just a couple of spoonfuls is enough in a covered container. This will produce enough steam to cook the vegetables. In some cases the liquid content should be increased – cake mixtures should be quite soft, for example – for other recipes the quantity of liquid may be less. Unlike conventional cooking methods there tends to be less time for the cooking liquid to evaporate, so follow the recipes carefully.

COVERING FOOD The majority of foods should be covered before cooking in the microwave – fish, vegetables, casseroles, rice, and stewed fruits. When cooking foods like bacon or chops, cover them with absorbent kitchen paper to stop spattering and to allow extra moisture to evaporate.

Big casserole dishes with lids are great but if you do not have a cover for the pot you are using, then substitute a dinner plate. Special microwave-proof cooking film can be used for covering food (do not use ordinary cling film) or roasting bags (with special plastic ties) can be used to contain food completely during cooking.

DEFROSTING FOOD Follow your manufacturer's instructions, since they know the oven best. In general terms, use a defrost or low power setting. Check the food fairly frequently to turn it or to break pieces apart as they defrost. Allow a standing period once the food is removed from the microwave to complete the defrosting process.

REHEATING FOOD As a general rule foods to be reheated should be covered – canned beans, cold cooked stews, meat in gravy, vegetables, casseroles and rice dishes can all be reheated successfully. The timing will depend on the quantity – the more you have the longer it will take. Check the food frequently and rearrange or turn it as necessary. Make sure that the food is properly reheated before it is eaten and allow a short period of standing time for temperatures of different foods to equalize before serving.

ARRANGING FOOD Whether defrosting, cooking or reheating, the food should be spread as far apart as possible in the dish to allow for even results. Arrange those parts which cook quickly towards the centre of the dish, or overlap them slightly, and put items or areas that need longest cooking towards the edge of the dish, or on top, where they will get the most energy.

REARRANGING FOOD When cooking dry items, turn and rearrange them at least once during cooking. Moist foods usually need less attention – casseroles need stirring, moving items from the outer edge of the dish into the middle – and some can be left with the minimum of attention given that the quantity of liquid and the size of the container are just right (for example, rice). Once you get to know your oven and have developed a repertoire of dishes, that you can cook confidently in the microwave, you should not have to spend ages turning and stirring everything you cook.

COOKING TIMES

Remember the more food you put in the microwave, the longer it will take to cook. Unfortunately, the variations in cooking time are not directly proportional to the variation in quantities of food – it is not as simple as doubling the time for twice the amount of food (it is usually about two-thirds to three-quarters, depending on the type of food). Dense foods take longer to cook or reheat than light foods and large portions of food require longer cooking than food which is cut into small pieces. The shape of the cooking container can also play a role in shortening the cooking time. Deep, narrow containers are often better than wide, shallow dishes, depending on the type of food that is cooked. For example, rice, casseroles and sauces benefit from being in a deep basin, or bowl, instead of being spread out over a large area where the middle will take longer to cook, and the food will have to be stirred to ensure even cooking. By contrast, several small items of food cook best if they are spread as far apart as possible in a large shallow dish.

Soups and Starters

The microwave is perfect for cooking starters – small individual dishes can be prepared speedily, or delicious pâtés can be made in advance. When it comes to making soup, you will find the microwave a great help. Remember not to add large quantities of cold liquid as this will result in lengthy cooking times. Instead add boiling water from the kettle or heat stocks before adding them to the soup (do this in the microwave while you prepare all the ingredients, or use stock cubes with boiling water).

● For chunky soups cook the ingredients in a small amount of liquid, then heat with the remaining stock or milk.

● For smooth soups, cook the ingredients first, then purée them and add the bulk of the hot liquid before heating through. Just before they are served you can always warm bread rolls in a basket for a few seconds in the microwave – delicious!

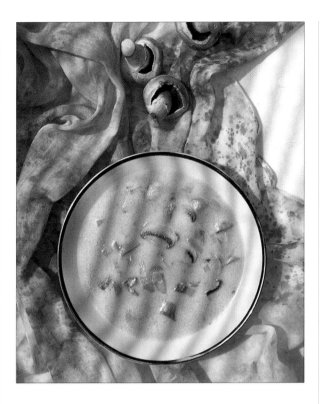

Mushroom Soup

SERVES 4

POWER SETTING: FULL

25 g/1 oz butter

1 onion, chopped

1 clove garlic, crushed

450 g/1 lb mushrooms, wiped and sliced

25 g/1 oz plain flour

600 ml/1 pt boiling vegetable stock

½ tsp dried thyme

1 bay leaf

2 parsley sprigs

50 ml/2 fl oz single cream

1 Place the butter, onion and garlic in a large bowl and cook on full for 3 minutes.

2 Add the mushrooms and cook on full for 3 minutes. Stir and cook for a further 2 minutes.

3 Stir in the flour, add half the vegetable stock, stir well and cook on full for 5 minutes.

4 Add the thyme, bay leaf, parsley and the remaining stock. Season well and cook on full for 10 minutes. Allow to stand for 5 minutes, then remove the bay leaf and parsley.

5 Stir in the cream and serve.

Leek and Potato Soup

SERVES 4

POWER SETTING: FULL

2 potatoes, diced

1 L/1¾ pt boiling vegetable stock

25 g/1 oz butter

1 onion, chopped

2 leeks, washed and sliced

2 tsp snipped chives

salt and freshly ground black pepper

1 bouquet garni

1 tbsp chopped parsley

1 Place the potatoes in a large bowl. Pour in the vegetables stock, cover and cook on full for 15 minutes, stirring once.

2 Place the butter, onion and leeks in a dish. Cook on full for 5 minutes, then add to the soup with the chives, seasoning and bouquet garni. Cook on full for 10 minutes. Taste for seasoning, checking that the vegetables are cooked. If not, cook for a further 2 minutes on full.

3 Sprinkle with chopped parsley and serve with slices of wholewheat bread.

Vichyssoise and Tomato, Carrot and Orange Soup

Vichyssoise

SERVES 4

POWER SETTING: FULL

350 g/12 oz potatoes, diced

1 onion, sliced

½ cucumber, peeled and diced

3 leeks, trimmed, washed and sliced

50 g/2 oz butter

4 tbsp water

1 L/1¾ pt boiling chicken stock

salt and freshly ground black pepper

150 ml/¼ pt single cream

2 tbsp snipped chives

1 Place the potatoes in a bowl with the onion, cucumber, leeks, butter and water. Cover and cook on full for 8–10 minutes, stirring once.

2 Add the stock and seasoning to taste. Cover and cook for a further 5 minutes or until the vegetables are tender. Cool slightly, then blend the soup in a blender or food processor until smooth.

3 Taste the soup and adjust the seasoning. Cool and chill, then serve the soup topped with cream and chives.

Tomato, Carrot and Orange Soup

SERVES 4

POWER SETTING: FULL

2 (425-g/15-oz) cans tomatoes, mashed with their juice

225 g/8 oz carrots, chopped

juice of 1 orange

1 bay leaf

600 ml/1 pt boiling chicken stock

finely grated rind of ½ orange

salt and freshly ground black pepper

150 ml/¼ pt single cream

1 Place the tomatoes, carrots, orange juice and bay leaf in a bowl. Cover and cook on full for 15 minutes, or until the carrots are tender, stirring once.

2 Remove the bay leaf and purée the vegetables in a blender or food processor. Return the purée to the bowl and pour in the stock. Add the orange rind and seasoning. Cook on full for 4 minutes until thoroughly heated, then serve topped with a generous swirl of cream. Alternatively, cool and chill the soup before serving.

Parsnip and Apple Soup

SERVES 4

POWER SETTING: FULL

25 g/1 oz butter

1 onion, chopped

450 g/1 lb parsnips, diced

225 g/8 oz cooking apples, peeled, cored and sliced

1 tsp dried mixed herbs

1 L/1¾ pt boiling vegetable stock

250 ml/8 fl oz single cream

1 tbsp chopped parsley

1 Place the butter and onion in a bowl and cook on full for 3 minutes.

2 Add the parsnips and cook on full for 3 minutes. Stir in the apple and herbs and cook for a further 2 minutes.

3 Pour in the stock and cook on full, covered, for 10 minutes. Allow to stand for a few minutes, then blend the soup until smooth in a blender or food processor.

4 Replace the soup in the bowl. Stir in the cream and cook on full for 5 minutes, but do not allow the soup to boil.

5 Serve sprinkled with chopped parsley, with wholewheat bread as an accompaniment.

Borscht

SERVES 4

POWER SETTING: FULL

450 g/1 lb beetroot, washed

4 tbsp water

3 spring onions, chopped

2 carrots, grated

2 potatoes, grated

1 bouquet garni

1 bay leaf

salt and freshly ground black pepper

1 L/1¾ pt boiling vegetable stock

2 courgettes

100 ml/4 fl oz natural yogurt

juice of 1 lemon

1 tbsp snipped chives

1 Trim the beetroot and remove any damaged skin. Place in a casserole, add the water and cook on full for 10 minutes, then allow to cool.

2 Grate the cooked beetroot and place in a large bowl with the vegetables, except the courgettes. Add the bouquet garni, bay leaf and seasoning. Pour in the stock, cover and cook on full for 18–20 minutes.

3 Cut the courgettes into thin strips, add to the soup and cook on full for a further 10 minutes. The vegetables should be tender. Cook for a little longer if they are still very crisp.

4 Serve either hot or cold. Mix the yogurt and lemon juice and serve swirled into the soup. Top with snipped chives.

Minestrone

SERVES 4

POWER SETTING: FULL

100 g/4 oz dried haricot beans, soaked overnight, then drained

1 L/1¾ pt boiling water

2 onions, finely chopped

2 carrots, chopped

1 small turnip, chopped

½ cauliflower, cut in florets

1 bouquet garni

1 bay leaf

1 vegetable stock cube

salt and freshly ground black pepper

1 leek, washed and sliced

¼ small cabbage, shredded

1 tbsp chopped parsley

grated Parmesan cheese to serve

1 Rinse the soaked beans under cold running water. Place in a large bowl or casserole with the boiling water. Cook on full for 15 minutes, or until the beans are tender.

2 Add the onions, carrots and turnip to the beans and cook on full for 8 minutes.

3 Then add the cauliflower florets, stir in the bouquet garni, bay leaf, vegetable stock cube and seasoning. Cook for a further 10 minutes on full.

4 Finally, add the leek and cabbage and cook for a further 8–12 minutes on full, or until the vegetables are tender.

5 Sprinkle the soup with chopped parsley and serve the Parmesan cheese separately.

Butter Bean and Mushroom Chowder

SERVES 4

POWER SETTING: FULL

100 g/4 oz dried butter beans

600 ml/1 pt boiling vegetable stock

25 g/1 oz butter

2 onions, chopped

2 sticks celery, sliced

225 g/8 oz potatoes, cubed

salt and freshly ground black pepper

100 g/4 oz mushrooms, sliced

1 (198-g/7-oz) can sweet corn

300 ml/½ pt milk

1 tbsp chopped parsley

1 Soak the beans in cold water overnight. Drain, rinse and place in a large bowl with the stock. Cover and cook on full for 20 minutes.

2 Place the butter, onions and celery in a bowl and cook for 4 minutes on full power. Add the potatoes, stir and cook for 5 minutes. Stir again, and cook on full for a further 3 minutes.

3 Add the vegetables to the beans and season well. Cook on full for 10 minutes, then leave to stand for 5 minutes.

4 Add the mushrooms, corn and milk. Cook on full for 10–12 minutes. Sprinkle with chopped parsley and serve with wholewheat bread.

Mediterranean Fish Soup

SERVES 4

POWER SETTING: FULL

4 tbsp olive oil

1 large onion, finely chopped

2 cloves garlic, crushed

2 sticks celery, sliced

2 (425-g/15-oz) cans tomatoes, chopped

150 ml/¼ pt dry white wine

600 ml/1 pt boiling water

salt and freshly ground black pepper

1.15 L/2 pt mussels, scrubbed and beards removed

225 g/8 oz white fish fillet, skinned

1 mackerel, skinned and filleted

100 g/4 oz peeled cooked prawns

parsley, chopped to garnish

1 Place the oil, onion and garlic in a bowl and cook on full for 4 minutes.

2 Add the celery and tomatoes, wine, water and seasoning. Cook on full for 15 minutes.

3 Ladle a little of the soup broth into a separate, large bowl and place the washed mussels in it. Cover and cook on full for 5–8 minutes, stirring once. Discard any unopened mussels, then add the rest to the soup.

4 Cut the white fish and mackerel into chunks, place in a dish, cover and cook on full for 3–4 minutes, or until firm. Add to the soup with the prawns. Cook on full for 1–2 minutes to heat before serving, garnish with chopped parsley.

Fish Chowder

SERVES 4

POWER SETTING: FULL

450 g/1 lb white fish fillet, skinned

25 g/1 oz butter

1 large onion, finely chopped

1–2 cloves garlic, crushed

4 potatoes, sliced

1 (425-g/14-oz) can tomatoes

2–3 thyme sprigs

2–3 parsley sprigs

1–2 bay leaves or 1 bouquet garni

salt and freshly ground black pepper

pinch of cayenne pepper

300 ml/½ pt boiling water

150 ml/¼ pt milk

8 plain crackers, crushed (optional)

2 tbsp chopped parsley

1 Remove any bones from the fish, then cut into even-sized chunks.

2 Place the butter, onion, garlic and potatoes in a bowl and cover. Cook on full for 15 minutes, or until the potatoes are almost tender.

3 Add the tomatoes, herbs and seasonings. Pour in the water, then gently stir in the fish.

4 Cover and cook on full for 8–10 minutes, or until the potatoes are cooked and the fish is firm. Stir halfway through the time to ensure even cooking.

5 Add the milk and heat on full for 1 minute but do not allow the soup to boil.

6 Place the crackers in the bottom of individual soup bowls, then ladle the soup on top. Sprinkle with chopped parsley and serve with warm French bread or crispy rolls. Alternatively, omit the crackers and serve the soup straight from the cooking dish.

MICROWAVE TIP

Large, microwave-proof glass dishes – casseroles or mixing bowls – are ideal for preparing soups in the microwave. If they do not have lids use dinner plates as covers.

Chicken Liver Pâté

SERVES 4
POWER SETTING: FULL
225 g/8 oz chicken livers, roughly chopped
1 small onion, chopped
2 cloves garlic, chopped
150 g/5 oz butter
2 tsp fresh chopped thyme or ½ tsp dried thyme
salt and freshly ground black pepper
1 tbsp port
1 tbsp single or double cream
GARNISH
fresh thyme sprigs
juniper berries

1 Place the chicken livers, onion, garlic, half the butter and the thyme in a bowl. Cover and cook on full for 5 minutes, stirring once. Cool slightly.

2 Purée the mixture in a blender or food processor, adding seasoning to taste, the port and cream. Divide the pâté between four individual pots or small dishes, smoothing the top evenly.

3 Place the remaining butter in a small bowl and cook on full for 30 seconds, or until melted. Pour the butter over the pâté, then chill thoroughly before serving. Garnish with fresh thyme and juniper berries and serve with crusty French bread.

Kipper Pâté

SERVES 4
POWER SETTING: MEDIUM
4 frozen kipper fillets
1 onion, finely chopped
25 g/1 oz butter
1 tbsp lemon juice
75 g/3 oz full-fat cream cheese
1 tbsp sherry
salt and freshly ground black pepper
parsley sprigs to garnish

1 Place the fish, onion, butter and lemon juice in a dish, cover and cook on medium for 8–10 minutes, turning and rearranging the fish once.

2 Remove all skin and any bones from the kipper fillets, flaking the fish. Purée the flaked kippers with the cooking juices and the onion, the cream cheese and sherry in a blender or food processor, then add seasoning to taste.

3 Divide the pâté between four individual dishes. Cool and chill well, then garnish with parsley sprigs. Serve with hot toast.

MICROWAVE TIP

Chicken livers, kidneys and other tender offal cook very well in the microwave. The thin membrane surrounding the livers should be pierced before cooking, or the livers should be cut up, to prevent them bursting during cooking. Always cover the cooking container when preparing livers to prevent spattering.

Mushroom Pâté

Mushroom Pâté

SERVES 4

POWER SETTING: FULL

50 g/2 oz butter

2 cloves garlic, crushed

225 g/8 oz mushroom caps, wiped and sliced

3 tbsp chopped parsley

50 g/2 oz fresh breadcrumbs

50 g/2 oz cheese, grated

¼ tsp grated nutmeg

salt and freshly ground black pepper

juice of 1 lemon

1 tbsp Cognac

2 tbsp double cream

parsley sprig to garnish

1 Place the butter, garlic and mushrooms in a bowl and cook on full for 6 minutes.

2 Add the parsley, breadcrumbs, cheese, nutmeg, seasoning, lemon juice, Cognac and cream to the mushrooms. Stir well and cook for a further 1 minute on full.

3 Blend all the ingredients in a blender or food processor and turn into a bowl. Allow to cool before chilling for 1 hour.

4 Garnish with parsley and serve with toast.

Individual Crab Soufflés

SERVES 3—6

POWER SETTINGS: FULL AND MEDIUM

25 g/1 oz butter

25 g/1 oz plain flour

salt and freshly ground black pepper

4 tbsp milk

2 egg yolks

1 (100-g/4-oz) can crab meat, drained and flaked

100 g/4 oz Gruyère cheese, grated

3 egg whites

a little paprika

1 Butter six individual dishes. Place the butter in a large bowl and cook on full for 1 minute. Stir in the flour and season, then continue to cook for 1–2 minutes.

2 Carefully blend in the milk and cook on full for 1–2 minutes, stirring once, until the sauce thickens.

3 Stir in the egg yolks, crab meat and cheese; allow to cool.

4 Whisk the egg whites until stiff and fold them into the mixture. Divide between the dishes, dust with paprika and cook on medium for 7–9 minutes, or until set. Serve at once.

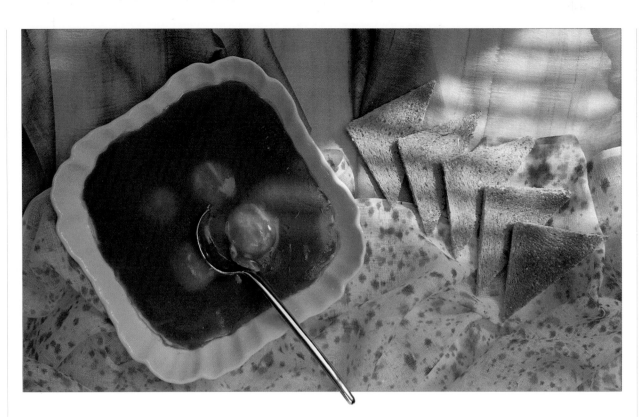

Poached Eggs with Red Wine Sauce

SERVES 4

POWER SETTING: FULL

2 leeks, white parts only, thinly sliced

2–3 tbsp water

50 g/2 oz butter

250 ml/8 fl oz red wine

salt and freshly ground black pepper

grated nutmeg

1 bouquet garni

25 g/1 oz plain flour

4 eggs

1 Put the leeks into a dish with the water and cook on full for 2 minutes; drain.

2 Melt one-third of the butter in a dish on full for 1 minute, add the leeks and stir well. Cook for a further 3 minutes on full.

3 Add the wine, seasoning, nutmeg and bouquet garni and cook on full for 5 minutes. Discard the bouquet garni.

4 Mix the flour with half the remaining butter until the mixture is crumbly. Add the butter and flour to the leeks in small pieces and whisk lightly until the mixture is smooth. Cook on full for 5 minutes, then check the sauce is smooth and well seasoned.

5 Place the remaining butter in a large dish. Melt on full for 30–45 seconds. Break the eggs into the dish, and prick their yolks with a skewer. Baste them with the butter. Cover and cook for 2 minutes. Allow to stand to finish cooking for about 30 seconds.

6 Reheat the sauce on full for 2 minutes, pour over the eggs and serve at once. Crisp toast makes a good accompaniment.

Stuffed Artichokes

18

Stuffed Artichokes

SERVES 4

POWER SETTING: FULL

| 4 globes artichokes |
| 4 tbsp water |
| grated rind and juice of 1 lemon |
| 25 g/1 oz fresh breadcrumbs |
| 100 g/4 oz mushrooms, chopped |
| salt and freshly ground black pepper |
| 1 spring onion, chopped |
| 50 ml/2 fl oz single cream |
| 4 slices Gruyère cheese |
| 25 g/1 oz butter |

1 Prepare the artichokes: cut off the stalks and remove the two rows of outer leaves with a sharp knife or scissors. Cut off about 2.5 cm/1 in from the top of each artichoke and trim the ends off all the remaining leaves.

2 Put the prepared artichokes in a covered casserole dish with the water and half the lemon juice. Cook on full for 20 minutes. Remove and drain upside down on a wire rack.

3 Push down with three fingers into the middle section of the leaves and pull these out, leaving the choke visible. Remove it with a teaspoon, making sure that you do not scrape away the artichoke bottom.

4 Mix the breadcrumbs with the finely grated lemon rind. Add the mushrooms, seasoning, and spring onion. Mix in the cream.

5 Stuff the artichoke hearts with the breadcrumb mixture and lay a slice of cheese on top of the stuffing. Place them on a dish, cover and cook on full for 5 minutes. Allow to stand for 2 minutes.

6 Melt the butter and mix it with the remaining lemon juice. Pour a little butter and lemon juice over each artichoke, and serve at once.

Corn-on-the-cob

SERVES 4

POWER SETTING: FULL

| 4 corn-on-the-cob with husks |
| 100 ml/4 fl oz water |
| 50 g/2 oz butter |
| 1 tbsp sliced green or black olives |
| 1 tsp capers, chopped |
| 2 spring onions, chopped |
| ½ red pepper, seeded and diced |
| 50 g/2 oz mushrooms, wiped and sliced |
| salt and freshly ground black pepper |

1 Place the corn in its husks in a bowl with the water. Cover and cook on full for 5 minutes, then leave to stand for 2 minutes.

2 Melt the butter in a bowl on full for 1 minute. Add all the other ingredients and continue to cook for 3 minutes.

3 Remove the husks from the corn and pour the butter mixture over the cobs. Season well and serve.

Corn-on-the-cob

Mushrooms à la Grecque

SERVES 4

POWER SETTING: FULL

2 lemons

250 ml/8 fl oz water

1 bouquet garni

1 bay leaf

6 peppercorns, lightly crushed

1 small onion, thinly sliced

¼ tsp soy sauce

450 g/1 lb button mushrooms, wiped

100 ml/4 fl oz white wine

freshly ground black pepper

1 tbsp olive oil

shreds of lemon rind to garnish

1 Thinly peel the rind from 1 lemon and place in a bowl with the water, bouquet garni, bay leaf, peppercorns, onion and soy sauce. Cook on full for 10 minutes, then allow to stand for 10 minutes to infuse.

2 Squeeze the juice of 1 lemon. Peel the other lemon and cut the flesh into thin slices. Remove the stalks from the mushrooms.

3 Arrange the mushrooms in a dish. Strain the lemon stock over the mushrooms. Add the lemon juice, wine, slices of lemon and a grind of black pepper. Cook on full for 6 minutes, allow to stand for 5 minutes, then cook for a further 6 minutes. Allow to cool.

4 Sprinkle the olive oil over the mushrooms and chill. Garnish with lemon rind and serve with crusty bread.

VARIATION

Leeks à la Grecque: Substitute trimmed and sliced leeks for the mushrooms. Cook as above.

Sweet Pepper Hors D'Oeuvre

SERVES 4

POWER SETTING: FULL

4 red, green or yellow peppers, seeded

50 ml/2 fl oz water

100 ml/4 oz vegetable oil

1 clove garlic, crushed

1 tsp dried marjoram

juice of 2 lemons

salt and freshly ground black pepper

1 Slice the peppers into thin strips and place in a flat dish. Avoid piling the strips on top of each other. Add the water and cook, covered, on full for 2 minutes. Drain.

2 Place the oil and garlic in a dish. Cook on full for 2 minutes. Add the pepper strips and marjoram and cook, covered, for 5 minutes on full.

3 Allow to cool, sprinkle with lemon juice and seasoning. Chill and serve as a starter or as a salad.

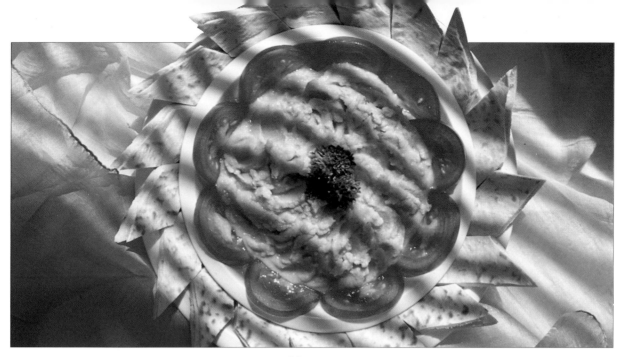

Hummus

Hummus

SERVES 4

POWER SETTING: FULL

225 g/8 oz chick peas, soaked overnight and drained

1 L/1¾ pt boiling water

1 bouquet garni

1 small onion, sliced

2 cloves garlic, crushed

juice of 2 lemons

50 g/2 oz tahini paste

4 tbsp olive oil

salt and freshly ground black pepper

GARNISH

parsley sprig

halved tomato slices

1 Place the peas in a large dish with the water, bouquet garni and onion. Cook, covered, on full for 20 minutes.

2 Leave to stand for 5 minutes, then cook on full, for a further 25 minutes, or until the peas are tender. Drain and allow to cool. Discard the bouquet garni.

3 Grind the peas to a paste with all the remaining ingredients in a blender or food processor.

4 Spoon the hummus into a dish and sprinkle with a little extra olive oil. Garnish and serve with warm pitta bread.

Paprika Mushrooms

SERVES 4

POWER SETTING: FULL

25 g/1 oz butter or margarine

1 onion, finely chopped

½ green pepper, seeded and finely chopped

1 tbsp paprika

350 g/12 oz mushrooms, sliced

150 ml/¼ pt soured cream

salt and freshly ground black pepper

parsley, chopped to garnish

1 Place the butter, onion and pepper in a large bowl and cook on full for 3 minutes.

2 Add the paprika and mushrooms, stir well and cook for a further 5 minutes. Stir in the soured cream, season to taste and warm through on full for 2 minutes.

3 Serve, sprinkled with parsley, with hot French bread. A crisp salad makes an excellent accompaniment.

COOK'S TIP

Tahini is a paste made from sesame seeds. It is usually beige in colour | and available in jars from health-food shops.

21

Salad Provençal

Salad Provençale

SERVES 4

POWER SETTING : FULL

459 g/1 lb whole green beans

5 tbsp water

4 spring onions

1 tsp dried thyme

1 green pepper, seeded

1 red pepper, seeded

4 tomatoes, peeled

4 hard-boiled eggs

100 ml/4 fl oz olive oil

1 tsp French mustard

4 tbsp wine vinegar

salt and freshly ground black pepper

1 clove garlic

1 lettuce

20 black olives

1 Trim the beans, arrange in a dish with 2 tbsp of the water. Cover and cook on full for 5 minutes.

2 Chop all but two of the spring onions finely. Add the chopped spring onions and thyme to the beans. Mix well and cook on full for another 5 minutes. Drain and allow to cool.

3 Slice the peppers into strips and arrange them in a shallow dish. Add the remaining water and cook for 5 minutes on full. Drain and allow to cool.

4 Cut each tomato into eight wedges and each egg into six wedges. To make the dressing, mix the oil, mustard, vinegar and seasoning in a screw-top jar and shake well.

5 Take a large salad bowl and rub it with a cut clove of garlic. Line with lettuce leaves, and put the beans mixed with half the dressing in the bottom of the bowl. Arrange the peppers, tomatoes and eggs on top with the black olives. Chop the reserved spring onions and sprinkle them over the dish. Add rest of the dressing just before serving. Serve with slices of wholewheat or French bread.

Fish and Seafood

Being tender, light and moist, fish and sea-food cook well in the microwave. Whole fish, fillets, steaks or chunks of fish can be cooked simply with butter and herbs or as part of a casserole, or in a sauce.

There are a few points to remember for success.

● Fish should be covered during cooking to keep it moist.

● Never sprinkle salt over fish before cooking – it can be cooked in seasoned sauces but plain cuts should not be salted as this will cause dehydrated spots on the cooked food.

● Arrange the thin parts of fish fillets towards the centre of the dish with the thicker parts towards the outside where they will cook best.

Overlap the tail ends of several fillets. Arrange steaks as far apart as possible and lay whole fish head to tail, turning them and swapping positions if there are more than two in the dish.

● Fish should be cooked until it is just firm and still very slightly undercooked as it comes out of the microwave. It is so hot that it will continued to cook on standing before serving.

● Most seafood is available ready cooked – prawns, lobster and crab – and it requires very brief heating in most recipes. Mussels cook particularly well in the microwave, so try the recipe for Moules à la Marinière on page 39 if you are a fan of this shellfish. The following chart provides a guide to cooking times for a selection of fish and seafood.

Fish and Shellfish Defrosting and Cooking Guide

FISH OR SHELLFISH	WEIGHT	DEFROSTING: MINUTES ON LOW	STANDING: MINUTES	COOKING: MINUTES ON FULL
bass	225 g/8 oz	5–6	15	5–6
bonito tuna steaks	225 g/8 oz	10	15	–
bream, sea-bream	225 g/8 oz	–	15	10–12
cod fillets	225 g/8 oz	4–5	5	4–6
cod steaks	225 g/8 oz	5	5	6
crab claws	100 g/4 oz	5	5	2–3
crab, dressed	100 g/4 oz	2	10	–
haddock fillets	100 g/4 oz	4–5	5	5–7
haddock steaks	100 g/4 oz	4–5	5	4–7
hake steaks	100 g/4 oz	4–5	5	4–6
halibut steaks	100 g/4 oz	4–5	5	4–5
kipper, whole	100 g/4 oz	–	–	1–2
kipper fillets (boil-in-the-bag)	200 g/7 oz	3	5	3
mackerel	225 g/8 oz	6–8	8–10	4–5
mullet, red and grey	225 g/8 oz	6–8	8–10	4–6
mussels	225 g/8 oz	5	5	–
plaice fillets	225 g/8 oz	4–5	5	4
prawns, peeled cooked	225 g/8 oz	5	5	–
red salmon steaks	225 g/8 oz	5	5	4–5
scampi, raw	225 g/8 oz	5	5	4–6
scallops	225 g/8 oz	5	5	5–7
scrod fillets	225 g/8 oz	4–5	30	4–5
snapper	225 g/8 oz	6–8	8–10	5–7
sole	225 g/8 oz	5–6	8–10	4
trout	225 g/8 oz	6–8	8–10	7

Fillets of Sole in Mustard Cream Sauce

SERVES 4

POWER SETTING: FULL

4 sole, filleted and skinned

1 small onion, chopped

1 small carrot, chopped

1 bay leaf

1 small glass dry white wine

150 ml/¼ pt water

25 g/1 oz butter

2 tbsp flour

salt and freshly ground black pepper

3 tbsp single cream

2 tsp made English mustard

fresh dill or parsley sprigs to garnish

1 Roll up the fish fillets and place them in a shallow dish with the onion, carrot, bay leaf, wine and water. Cover and cook on full for 5 minutes. Drain and reserve the liquid, discarding the vegetables and bay leaf.

2 Place the butter in a bowl and cook on full for 1 minute. Stir in the flour, then gradually add the fish liquor. Cook for a further 3 minutes, until thickened, stirring every minute.

3 Stir in seasoning to taste, the cream and mustard and pour the sauce over the fish. Cook on full for 1 minute before serving, garnished with dill or parsley.

COOK'S TIP

The fish is delicious served with a piped potato accompaniment. Pipe mashed potatoes around the edge of a dish and brown under the grill. Serve the fish in the middle.

Fillets of Sole in White Wine
with Mushrooms

SERVES 4

POWER SETTING: FULL

4 lemon sole, filleted and skinned

150 ml/¼ pt dry white wine

150 ml/¼ pt boiling water

1 small onion, sliced

6 button mushrooms

1 bay leaf

parsley sprig

4 peppercorns

15 g/½ oz butter

15 g/½ oz plain flour

salt and freshly ground white pepper

2 tbsp single cream

GARNISH

lemon slices

parsley sprigs

1 Roll up the fish fillets from head to tail and arrange them in a shallow dish.

2 Pour over the wine and water, then add the onion, mushroom stalks, herbs and peppercorns. Cover and cook on full for 7–9 minutes, rearranging halfway through cooking. Strain the cooking liquid.

3 Place the mushrooms caps and the butter in a basin and cook on full for 2 minutes, stir then cook for a further 1 minute. Use a slotted spoon to remove the mushrooms and set aside.

4 Stir the flour into the juices in the basin then whisk in the cooking liquid from the fish. Cook on full for 4–5 minutes, whisking once, until the sauce is thickened and boiling. Season to taste.

5 Add the cream to the sauce. Pour the sauce over the fish, add the reserved mushrooms to the dish and cook on full for 1 minute to reheat.

6 Serve at once, garnished with lemon and parsley.

MICROWAVE TIP

When cooking fish fillets in the microwave, best results are obtained by rolling or folding them. Arrange the fish rolls in a shallow dish, as far apart as possible and towards the outside edge of the dish. Cover the fish before cooking – for this use special microwave cling film, or an upturned dinner plate usually works equally well with a round dish. Turn the fish rolls over halfway through cooking and, if the dish is fairly full, re-position them.

Fillets of Sole in Mustard Cream Sauce

Sole Dugléré

SERVES 4

POWER SETTING: FULL

50 g/2 oz butter

1 onion, chopped

3 tomatoes, peeled and chopped

8 sole fillets

150 ml/¼ pt white wine

15 g/½ oz plain flour

salt and freshly ground black pepper

GARNISH

1 tomato, peeled and sliced

parsley sprigs

1 Place half the butter and the onion in a shallow dish and cook on full for 4 minutes. Add the tomatoes, stir and cook on full for 3 minutes.

2 Fold the fish fillets in three and lay on top of the tomato and onion mixture, add the wine and cover. Cook on full for 3–5 minutes or until the fish is firm.

3 Remove the fish to a serving dish and keep warm.

4 Cream the remaining butter and flour in a basin, then stir in the sieved cooking liquid to make a sauce. Cook on full for 3–4 minutes, until boiling and thickened. Season to taste.

5 Pour the sauce over the fish and garnish with sliced tomatoes and parsley sprigs.

> **COOK'S TIP**
>
> Serve the delicate, microwave-cooked fish with crisp Duchesse potatoes, cooked in the conventional oven. To peel tomatoes, place them in a basin and pour on boiling water to cover. Leave for 30–60 seconds, then split the skins with a knife and they slide off easily.

Cod with Courgettes

SERVES 4

POWER SETTING: FULL

4 cod cutlets

juice of 1 lemon

75 g/3 oz butter

1 onion, thinly sliced

4 courgettes, chopped

1 (50-g/2-oz) can anchovy fillets, drained

1 tbsp capers

freshly ground black pepper

lemon slices

1 Place the fish in a large shallow dish and sprinkle with the lemon juice. Cover and cook on full for 3 minutes. Turn the cutlets over and set aside.

2 Place the butter in a dish and cook for 1 minute. Add the onion and courgettes and cook for 3 minutes, then stir in the anchovies and capers. Season with pepper and spoon the mixture over the fish.

3 Cover and cook on full for 3 minutes, until the cutlets are just cooked. The exact time depends on the size of the fish cutlets. Garnish with lemon slices and serve with mashed potato.

Suffolk Fish Pie

SERVES 4–6
POWER SETTING: FULL
450 g/1 lb smoked fish fillets, skinned and cut into chunks
3 medium leeks, trimmed, washed and sliced
175 g/6 oz peeled cooked prawns
3 tbsp water
675 g/1½ lb potatoes, cubed
25 g/1 oz butter
a little milk
1 tbsp grated Parmesan cheese
SAUCE
250 ml/8 fl oz milk
25 g/1 oz butter
25 g/1 oz plain flour
salt and freshly ground black pepper
50 g/2 oz Edam cheese, grated
parsley sprigs to garnish

1 Place the smoked fish in a bowl, cover and cook on full for 4 minutes, or until firm. Transfer to a deep pie dish. Add the leeks to any leftover juices, cover and cook on full for 4–5 minutes, until tender. Use a slotted spoon to transfer the leeks to the pie dish, reserving the cooking liquor. Add the prawns to the fish and leeks and mix lightly.

2 Place the water and potatoes in a large bowl. Cover and cook on full for 10 minutes, then set aside, still covered for 10 minutes.

3 To make the sauce, mix the reserved cooking liquor with the milk. Place the butter in a bowl and cook on full for 30 seconds, then stir in the flour and milk. Cook for a further 3 minutes, whisking twice, until boiling and thickened. Season the sauce to taste, stir in the cheese, then pour it over the fish mixture in the pie dish.

4 Drain and mash the potatoes with the butter and a little milk. Season to taste, then spread them over the fish mixture. Sprinkle with the Parmesan and cook, uncovered on full, for 4 minutes, until hot.

5 If you like, brown the pie under a hot grill before serving garnished with parsley sprigs.

Portuguese Fish Casserole with Rice

SERVES 4

POWERSETTINGS: FULL AND MEDIUM-HIGH

5 tbsp olive oil

1 tbsp cider vinegar

salt and freshly ground black pepper

1 kg/2 lb white fish fillet, skinned and cut into chunks

1 large onion, sliced

1 large green pepper, seeded and cut into chunks

1 large red pepper, seeded and cut into chunks

2–3 cloves garlic, chopped

175 g/6 oz long-grain rice

450 ml/¾ pt boiling fish stock or water

1 (425-g/15-oz) can tomatoes, mashed with their juice

GARNISH

tomato wedges

chopped parsley

Portuguese Fish Casserole with Rice

1 Mix 3 tbsp of the oil with the vinegar and seasoning. Put the fish in a large bowl and pour over the dressing. Add half the onion, peppers and garlic, mix and marinate for 30 minutes.

2 Place the remaining oil, onion, garlic and peppers in a bowl. Cover and cook on full for 3–4 minutes, until onion is transparent. Add the rice and fish stock or water, stir, cover and cook on full for 7 minutes.

3 Drain the rice, reserving the cooking liquor, then mix it with the fish and vegetables in a casserole. Add the tomatoes and enough of the reserved stock to just cover the ingredients.

4 Cover the casserole and cook on medium-high for 15 minutes or until the rice is tender and the fish is cooked. Allow to stand for 10 minutes before serving, garnished with tomato wedges and chopped parsley.

Haddock in Sweet and Sour Sauce

Haddock in Sweet and Sour Sauce

SERVES 2–4

POWER SETTING: FULL

1 tbsp minced onion

1 clove garlic, crushed

2 red chillies, seeded and finely sliced

1 slice fresh root ginger, grated

3 tbsp sherry

4 haddock fillets (about 450 g/1 lb total weight)

1 (200 g/7 oz) can tomatoes, drained and sieved

1 tbsp tomato purée

pinch of sugar

GARNISH

finely shredded spring onions

tomato slices

1 Mix the onion, garlic, chillies, ginger and sherry. Lay the fish in this marinade and leave for 1 hour, turning occasionally.

2 Mix the sieved tomatoes, tomato purée and sugar, and pour over the fish and its marinade. Cover and cook for about 5 minutes, turning once, until the fish is just cooked.

3 Garnish with finely shredded spring onions and tomato slices, and serve with plain cooked rice.

Kedgeree

SERVES 3–4

POWER SETTING: FULL

225 g/8 oz smoked haddock

150 ml/¼ pt milk

1 bay leaf

1 slice onion

salt and freshly ground black pepper

100 g/4 oz long-grain rice

pinch of turmeric

300 ml/½ pt boiling water

3 hard-boiled eggs

GARNISH

1 tbsp chopped parsley

½ tsp paprika

1 lemon slice

1 Place the fish in a dish with the milk, bay leaf, onion and a little pepper. Cover and cook on full for 5 minutes. Allow to cool slightly in the milk. Remove and flake the fish from the skin, discarding bones.

2 Place the rice, turmeric and water in a bowl, then strain in the cooking liquid from the fish. Cover and cook on full for 15–20 minutes, or until the liquid has been absorbed.

3 Add the fish to the rice. Chop 2 eggs and mix into the kedgeree with seasoning to taste.

4 Sieve the yolk of the remaining egg and chop the white, then use to garnish the kedgeree. Add chopped parsley, paprika and a slice of lemon to complete the garnish.

Kedgeree

Trout with Almonds

Fish with Sorrel Sauce

SERVES 4

POWER SETTING: FULL

675 g/1½ lb white fish fillet

1 shallot, finely chopped

75 ml/3 fl oz plus 1 tbsp water

75 ml/3 fl oz dry white wine

salt and freshly ground black pepper

100 g/4 oz sorrel or spinach, washed and trimmed

150 ml/¼ pt soured cream or natural yogurt

2 tsp cornflour

1 Place the fish in a shallow dish with the shallot, 75 ml/3 fl oz water, wine, salt and pepper. Cover and cook on full for 5–6 minutes, rearranging halfway through cooking. Set aside, still covered.

2 Shake the water off the sorrel and put it in a bowl. Cover and cook on full for 3–4 minutes: it should almost melt to softness when cooked. Blend the cooked sorrel with the soured cream in a blender or food processor to make a smooth sauce. (It is not necessary to drain the sorrel.)

3 Mix the cornflour with the strained cooking liquid from the fish. Cook on full for 3 minutes or until boiling and thickened.

4 Add the sorrel mixture and warm the sauce on full for 30–60 seconds. Spoon over the fish and serve immediately.

Trout with Almonds

SERVES 4

POWER SETTING: FULL

50 g/2 oz butter

50 g/2 oz flaked almonds

juice of ½ lemon

4 trout, cleaned, with heads on

salt and freshly ground black pepper

GARNISH

parsley sprigs

lemon wedges

1 Place the butter in a large oblong or oval dish. Cook on full for 1 minute. Stir in the almonds and cook for a further 1 minute.

2 Stir in the lemon juice, add the fish and baste. Sprinkle with pepper. Cover and cook on full for 2–3 minutes.

3 Turn the fish over and rearrange for even cooking. Baste with the cooking juices, then cook for a further 2–3 minutes, until all four fish are just cooked: the exact time depends on the size of the fish.

4 Transfer the fish to a warmed serving dish and season the juices lightly with salt. Spoon the almonds and juices over the fish, then garnish with parsley sprigs and lemon wedges before serving.

Trout Chaudfroid

SERVES 4

POWER SETTING: FULL

4 trout, cleaned and heads removed

2 tbsp water

1 tsp gelatine

250 ml/8 fl oz Béchamel Sauce (see page 111)

50 ml/2 fl oz aspic jelly

GARNISH

cucumber peel

canned pimiento

stuffed olives, sliced

watercress

salad ingredients

1 Place the fish in a dish. Cover and cook on full for 4–6 minutes, turning and re-arranging the fish halfway through cooking. Leave to cool, still covered.

2 Place the water in a small bowl and heat on full for 15–20 seconds, or until hot but not boiling.

Sprinkle the gelatine over, leave for 2 minutes to soften, then stir until dissolved completely. Stir the dissolved gelatine into the Béchamel sauce with the aspic.

3 Remove the skin from the fish. Lift the top fillet from the fish and remove the bone. Lay the fillet back on the fish.

4 Coat with the prepared sauce. Garnish with cucumber peel, cut into thin strips, diamond-shaped pieces of pimiento, and sliced stuffed olives to make flowers and leaves. Chill until set, then garnish with watercress and salad ingredients.

MICROWAVE TIP

Before cooking, make sure that the dish will fit into the microwave, without knocking the side walls if there is a turntable in the oven. The trout can be cooked in pairs, in a flan dish, allowing about two-thirds of the time suggested above. Wrap the first pair in foil, shiny side inwards, when cooked, to keep hot while the second pair of trout are cooked.

Mackerel with Oranges

Mackerel with Oranges

SERVES 4

POWER SETTING: FULL

4 mackerel, cleaned, heads and tails off

150 ml/¼ pt oil

150 ml/¼ pt fresh orange juice

grated rind of 1 orange

a few drops of Tabasco sauce

salt and freshly ground black pepper

50 g/2 oz black olives, stoned

GARNISH

orange slices

1 Using a sharp knife, make slanting incisions across both sides of each fish. Place in a large shallow dish.

2 Mix the oil, orange juice, rind and Tabasco and season with salt and pepper. Pour the mixture over the fish and marinate for 2 hours, turning occasionally.

3 Baste the fish, add the olives and cover the dish, then cook on full for 2–3 minutes. Turn and rearrange the fish, then cook for a further 2–3 minutes, depending on the size of the fish. Serve the fish with the juices spooned over it, garnished with orange slices.

Red Mullet on a Bed of Shredded Vegetables

SERVES 4

POWER SETTING: FULL

4 red mullet (about 175 g/6 oz each), scaled and gutted

juice of 1 lemon

2 tbsp water

225 g/8 oz carrots, cut into matchstick strips

225 g/8 oz white cabbage, finely shredded

1 tbsp juniper berries

1 tbsp clear honey

snipped chives to garnish

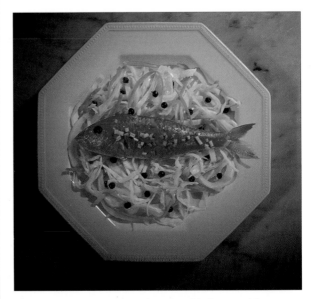

Red Mullet on a Bed of Shredded Vegetables

1 Put the fish in a dish with 1 tbsp of the lemon juice mixed with the water. Cover and cook on full for 4 minutes, turning once. Keep warm.

2 Mix the carrots, cabbage and juniper berries in a bowl. Pour over the remaining lemon juice and honey, and toss well. Cover and cook on full for about 3 minutes, until the vegetables are tender but not too soft.

3 Arrange the vegetables on four heated serving plates and lay the fish on top. Garnish with snipped chives and serve at once.

COOK'S TIP

Juniper berries are small, round and dark in colour – about the same size as peppercorns. They are a main	ingredient in the preparation of gin and give a similar – although less pronounced – flavour in cooking.

Red Mullet Provençal

SERVES 2

POWER SETTING: FULL

4 red mullet, cleaned with heads on

25 g/1 oz butter

300 ml/½ pt Tomato Sauce (see page 111)

1 green or red pepper, seeded and diced

1 tbsp port or sherry

salt and freshly ground black pepper

2 tbsp stoned black olives

GARNISH

lemon slices

watercress sprigs

1 Place the fish in a large shallow dish and dot with the butter. Cover and cook on full for 2 minutes. Turn and rearrange the fish.

2 Mix the tomato sauce with the diced pepper and the port or sherry. Pour the sauce over the fish, re-cover and cook for a further 2–4 minutes. The cooking time will depend on how hot the tomato sauce is. Check to make sure that the fish are cooked, turning them over in the sauce and allowing an extra 1–2 minutes if necessary.

3 Season the sauce, sprinkle the olives over the fish, then garnish with lemon slices and watercress.

Red Mullet Provençal

Soused Herring

SERVES 4

POWER SETTING: FULL

4 herrings, filleted

150 ml/¼ pt cider vinegar

150 ml/¼ pt water

½ tsp pickling spice

1 bay leaf

1 large cooking apple, peeled, cored and sliced

1 onion, sliced

salt and freshly ground black pepper

1 Roll up the fillets and secure them with wooden cocktail sticks.

2 Place the fish in a shallow dish with the vinegar, water, pickling spice and bay leaf. Top with the apple and onion.

3 Cover and cook on full for 8 minutes, rearranging the fish once. Add seasoning to taste, then allow to cool.

4 Chill and drain before serving with salad and new potatoes.

Soused Herring

Red Snapper à la Créole

SERVES 4

POWER SETTING: FULL

1–1.5 kg/2–3 lb red snapper, cleaned

juice of 1 lemon

few thyme sprigs

1 bay leaf

parsley sprig

4 allspice berries, crushed

4 cloves

STUFFING

½ onion, finely chopped

25 g/1 oz butter

2 tbsp fresh breadcrumbs

1 tbsp chopped parsley

salt and freshly ground black pepper

SAUCE

150 ml/¼ pt dry white wine

25 g/1 oz butter

1 green pepper, seeded and chopped

1 large onion, peeled and finely chopped

2 large tomatoes, peeled and chopped

100 g/4 oz mushrooms, stalks removed, sliced

1 (425-g/15-oz) can tomatoes

1 tbsp chopped parsley

parsley sprigs to garnish (optional)

1 Sprinkle the fish inside and out with lemon juice. Make an S-shaped cut in the back and fill with thyme, bay leaf, parsley, allspice and cloves.

2 For the stuffing, place the onion in a basin with the butter and cook on full for 2 minutes. Chop the mushroom stalks (from the sauce ingredients), add to the onion and cook for a further 2 minutes.

3 Stir the breadcrumbs, parsley and seasoning into the onion mixture and put the stuffing into the body of the fish.

4 Lay the fish in a flat dish and pour over the wine for the sauce. Cover and cook on full for 4 minutes, turning the fish over halfway through cooking.

5 For the sauce, place the butter, green pepper and onion in a basin and cook on full for 3 minutes. Add the fresh tomatoes and sliced mushrooms and cook for a further 3 minutes on full. Stir in the canned tomatoes, season and cook on full for 5 minutes.

6 Carefully, strain any cooking liquor from the fish into the sauce, then pour over the fish, heat on full for 1 minute and serve sprinkled with chopped parsley. Garnish with parsley sprigs if you like.

Skate in Caper Sauce

SERVES 4

POWER SETTING: FULL

4 wings skate

300 ml/½ pt boiling water

1 tbsp vinegar

1 small onion, sliced

1 bay leaf

15 g/½ oz butter

15 g/½ oz flour

3 tbsp capers, chopped

2 tbsp chopped parsley

salt and freshly ground black pepper

GARNISH

parsley sprigs

lemon slices

1 Place the fish in a large shallow dish. Mix the water, vinegar, sliced onion and bay leaf and pour over the fish.

2 Cover and cook on full for 2 minutes. Turn and rearrange the fish, then cook for a further 3–5 minutes, or until the fish is cooked.

3 In a basin cream the butter and flour, then gradually whisk in 300 ml/½ pt of cooking liquor from the fish. Cook on full for 4 minutes, whisking once, until boiling and thickened.

4 Add the capers, parsley and seasoning to taste. Drain any remaining liquid from the fish. Discard the onion and bay leaf and pour the sauce over. Reheat on full for 1–2 minutes, if necessary, then serve garnished with parsley and lemon.

Salmon Steaks with Hollandaise Sauce

SERVES 2

POWER SETTINGS: MEDIUM AND FULL

100 g/4 oz butter, diced

2 tbsp lemon juice

3 egg yolks

salt and freshly ground white pepper

4 salmon steaks (about 175 g/6 oz each)

1 Put the butter in a bowl and cook on medium for 2 minutes, or until melted. Add the lemon juice and the egg yolks and whisk lightly.

2 Cook on medium for 1 minute, whisk again and season to taste. Transfer the sauce to a heated jug and keep warm while you cook the salmon.

3 Place the fish steaks in a shallow dish. Cover and cook on full for 3½–4 minutes, rearranging the steaks and turning them over once during cooking. Serve with the sauce poured over.

> **COOK'S TIP**
>
> The salmon steaks can be served cold but they should not be chilled before serving. If cooling the fish, then make the sauce just before it is to be served. New potatoes and young peas make a good accompaniment.

Salmon Steaks with Hollandaise Sauce

Poached Salmon

Poached Salmon

SERVES 6

POWER SETTING: FULL

1 (1.25-kg/2-lb) salmon or salmon trout, cleaned with
head and tail on

3 tbsp water

GARNISH

300 ml/½ pt aspic jelly

½ cucumber, sliced

50 g/2 oz stuffed green olives, sliced

50 g/2 oz whole cooked prawns

lemon slices

watercress

1 Descale the fish and make one or two shallow cuts into the skin to prevent it from popping during cooking. Then place it in a large shallow dish or on a large plate. If you cannot fit the fish flat on a suitable dish for use in the microwave, then curve it in a large round flan dish. Sprinkle the water over the fish and cover it with microwave-proof cling film. If the fish is curved in a dish you will have to cover it with two layers of film to keep it in shape. Pierce the film in two or three places.

2 Cook on full for 7–10 minutes, turning the fish over halfway through cooking. If the fish is curved you will not be able to turn it but you should change the position of the dish in the oven to aid even cooking.

3 Leave the fish to cool, still covered. When cold, carefully remove the skin and lay the fish on a serving platter. Coat with a little aspic and garnish with cucumber and olive slices. Leave to set and chill the remaining aspic.

4 To serve, chop the chilled aspic, arrange it on the platter with the fish. Garnish with prawns, lemon and watercress. Serve with mayonnaise.

Salmon Mousse

Salmon Mousse

POWER SETTING: FULL

225–350 g/8–12 oz fresh salmon

2 parsley sprigs

1 bay leaf

1 slice onion

150 ml/¼ pt plus 3 tbsp water

300 ml/½ pt Béchamel Sauce (see page 111)

3 tsp gelatine

300 ml/½ pt mayonnaise

2–3 drops Tabasco sauce

1 tbsp tomato ketchup

salt and freshly ground white pepper

3–4 tbsp double or whipping cream, lightly whipped

50 g/2 oz peeled cooked prawns (optional)

2 egg whites

1 green pepper, seeded and chopped

150 ml/¼ pt aspic jelly

1 tsp tomato purée (optional)

salad ingredients to garnish

1 Place the fish in a dish with the parsley, bay leaf, onion and 150 ml/¼ pt water. Cover and cook on full for 3–5 minutes, or until the fish is just cooked. Leave to cool, still covered.

2 Drain the fish and use the liquor to make up the Béchamel sauce. Discard the onion, bay leaf and parsley. Flake fish, discarding skin and bone.

3 Heat the 3 tbsp water in a basin on full for 20–30 seconds, or until hot but not boiling. Sprinkle in the gelatine, leave for 2 minutes to soften, then stir until completely dissolved.

4 Mix the Béchamel sauce, fish, half the mayonnaise, Tabasco, tomato ketchup and seasoning. Stir in gelatine, cream and prawns (if used).

5 Whisk the egg whites until they stand in soft peaks. With a metal spoon, fold them into the fish. Turn into an oiled mould. Chill to set.

6 Turn out onto a serving plate. Mix the remaining mayonnaise with the aspic jelly and the tomato puree if used.

7 Coat the mousse with the mayonnaise mixture and allow to set. Garnish with salad ingredients.

Prawns St Jacques

SERVES 4

POWER SETTING: FULL

40 g/1½ oz butter

40 g/1½ oz plain flour

150 ml/¼ pt milk

150 ml/¼ pt single cream

4 tbsp grated Parmesan cheese

salt and freshly ground black pepper

450 g/1 lb peeled cooked prawns

450 g/1 lb cooked potato, mashed

2 tbsp grated Parmesan cheese

1 tbsp golden breadcrumbs

GARNISH

chopped parsley

lemon twists

4 whole cooked prawns

1 Put the butter in a bowl and cook on full for 1½ minutes, until melted. Stir in the flour and continue to cook for 1 minute. Stir in the milk and cook a further 1 minute, then stir in the cream and cook on full for 1 minute. Stir in the cheese and cook on full for 1 minute. Season the sauce to taste and whisk, or stir until smooth.

2 Stir the prawns into the sauce and divide between four scallop shells or shell-shaped dishes. Top with the mashed potato and sprinkle with Parmesan cheese, golden breadcrumbs and parsley. Heat through on full for 1 minute.

3 Garnish with parsley, lemon twists and the unshelled prawns and serve hot.

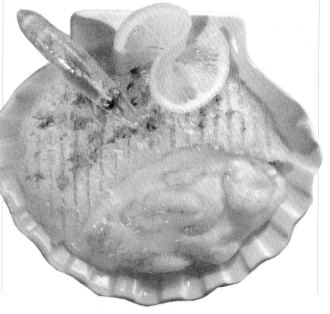

Prawn Curry

SERVES 4

POWER SETTING: FULL

1 onion, finely chopped

2 cloves garlic, crushed

1–2 tbsp oil

2 small potatoes, thinly sliced

2 tbsp curry powder

1 (425-g/15-oz) can tomatoes

1 tbsp tomato purée

300 ml/½ pt boiling fish stock or water

175 g/6 oz button mushrooms, stalks removed and chopped, caps left whole

1 bay leaf

1 bouquet garni

½ cauliflower, broken into florets

350 g/12 oz peeled cooked prawns

1 tbsp lemon juice

salt and freshly ground black pepper

1 Place the onion, garlic and oil in a dish and cook on full for 3–4 minutes, until the onion is transparent. Add the potatoes, cover and cook for 6–8 minutes, until half cooked.

2 Add the curry powder to the dish and mix with the other ingredients. Cover and cook on full for 2 minutes.

3 Add the tomatoes, purée and fish stock or water, mushroom stalks, bay leaf and bouquet garni. Cover and cook on full for 2 minutes.

4 Add the cauliflower, mushroom caps and stir. Cover and cook on full for a further 5–8 minutes, until the cauliflower is tender.

5 Add the prawns and lemon juice and cook on full for a further 5 minutes. Season to taste and serve with cooked rice, poppadums and chutneys.

Moules à la Marinière

SERVES 2

POWER SETTING: FULL

1.15 L/2 pt mussels

50 g/2 oz butter

1 onion, chopped

1 clove garlic, chopped

a handful of fresh parsley, chopped

freshly ground black pepper

1 glass dry white wine

1 Scrub the mussels under cold running water and scrape away the beards – the bunch of black threads that protrudes from the shell. Discard any mussels that are open or broken.

2 Place the butter in a large bowl and cook on full for 1 minute. Add the onion, garlic, parsley, pepper and wine. Cover and cook for 2 minutes.

3 Add the mussels, cover and continue to cook on full for about 3 minutes, or until the shells are open. Give the mussels a good stir halfway through cooking. Discard any mussels that have not opened.

4 Serve with French bread to mop up the cooking juices and provide a dish for the discarded shells.

Prawns in Whisky

SERVES 4

POWER SETTING: FULL

50 g/2 oz butter

1 small onion, chopped

350 ml/12 oz peeled cooked prawns

4 tbsp whipping cream

4 tbsp whisky

GARNISH

2 tbsp chopped parsley

2 lemon slices, quartered

8 whole cooked prawns

1 Place the butter in a dish and cook on full for 1 minute. Add the onion and continue to cook for 3 minutes.

2 Stir in the prawns and cook on full for 2–3 minutes, or until hot. Divide between four small warmed dishes.

3 Mix the cream and whisky in a small dish and cook on full for 30 seconds. Pour the sauce over the prawns. Garnish with the parsley, lemon and whole prawns and serve at one.

Prawns in Whisky

Scallops with Mushrooms

SERVES 4

POWER SETTING: FULL

150 ml/¼ pt dry white wine

150 ml/¼ pt boiling water

1 small onion, sliced

4 peppercorns

1 bay leaf

1 parsley sprig

100 g/4 oz mushrooms

50 g/2 oz butter

8 spring onions, chopped

2 tomatoes, peeled and chopped

8 scallops, cleaned and sliced

20 g/¾ oz plain flour

1 egg yolk

1 tbsp single cream

few drops of lemon juice

2 tbsp dry white breadcrumbs

GARNISH

lemon wedges

parsley sprigs

1 Place the first six ingredients in a bowl and cook on full for 7 minutes.

2 Remove the mushroom stalks and chop finely. Slice the caps, retaining 16 slices for garnish.

3 Place half the butter in a dish with the spring onions and mushroom stalks and cook on full for 4 minutes. Add the tomatoes and cook for a further 3 minutes.

4 Strain the wine mixture over the scallops in a basin. Cover and cook on full for 3–4 minutes. Remove the scallops with a slotted spoon, then add the mushroom slices to the cooking liquid and cook on full for 2 minutes. Strain the liquid and make up to 300 ml/½ pt with wine or water.

5 Beat the remaining butter and flour to a paste with a little of the cooling liquor, then whisk in the remaining liquid. Cook on full for 4 minutes, whisking once, until thickened and boiling. Whisk in the egg yolk and cream. Cook on full for 30 seconds, then add the sliced mushrooms.

6 Place the tomato mixture in four shells or one large dish.

7 Add the scallops to the mushroom sauce, taste for seasoning and add a few drops of lemon juice to taste. Pour into the shells or serving dish. Sprinkle with crumbs and garnish with the reserved mushroom slices. Heat through on full for 1 minute, then brown under a hot grill.

8 Serve garnished with lemon wedges and parsley.

Tuna, Corn and Pepper Flan

Tuna, Corn and Pepper Flan

SERVES 6

POWER SETTINGS: FULL AND MEDIUM

25 g/1 oz butter

25 g/1 oz plain flour

150 ml/¼ pt milk

1 (198-g/7-oz) can sweetcorn with peppers, drained

1 (198-g/7-oz) can tuna, drained and flaked

2 large eggs, beaten

salt and freshly ground black pepper

100 g/4 oz Edam cheese, grated

1 (18-cm/7-in) round cooked pastry case

GARNISH

red pepper rings

lemon balm or mint sprigs

1 Place the butter in a large bowl and cook on full for 1 minute. Add the flour, then gradually stir in the milk. Cover and cook on full for 3 minutes.

2 Add the corn with peppers and the tuna, then stir in the eggs, seasoning and cheese.

Oriental Crab Meat Salad

3 Pour the mixture into the pastry case and cook on medium for 5 minutes. Leave to stand for 5 minutes. Cook on full for a further 8 minutes or until the filling has nearly set. Allow to stand for 5 minutes before serving, garnished with red pepper and lemon balm or mint.

Oriental Crab Meat Salad

SERVES 4
POWER SETTING: FULL
225 g/8 oz long-grain rice
600 ml/1 pt boiling water
1 red pepper, seeded and sliced
1 green pepper, seeded and sliced
1-cm/½-in piece fresh root ginger, grated
1 (100-g/4-oz) can bean sprouts, drained
2 tbsp soy sauce
1 (200-g/7-oz) can crab meat or meat from 1 fresh cooked crab
150 ml/¼ pt vinaigrette dressing (see Cook's Tip, page 98)

1 Place the rice and water in a bowl. Cover and cook on full for 15–20 minutes, until all the water has been absorbed. Leave to cool.

2 Place the peppers in a basin and cook on full for 3 minutes. Place in a sieve and cool under cold water.

3 Mix the grated ginger with the bean sprouts and soy sauce in a basin and cook on full for 2 minutes.

4 Mix all the prepared ingredients and crab meat with the rice and toss in the vinaigrette dressing.

COOK'S TIP

This mixture can be served hot without the vinaigrette dressing: mix all the prepared ingredients into the hot rice. Heat on full for about 4–5 minutes.

Squid with Beetroot

SERVES 4

POWER SETTING: FULL

450 g/1 lb small squid

1 tbsp olive oil

1 small onion, chopped

1 clove garlic, crushed

1 stick celery, finely chopped

2 cooked beetroot, chopped

½ glass dry white wine

1 tbsp tomato purée

salt and freshly ground black pepper

celery leaves to garnish

1 Clean the squid: remove the eyes, mouth, ink sac and outer membrane. Take out the cuttlefish bone. Wash the squid well, then slice the body and tentacles.

2 Put the olive oil in a bowl and cook on full for 30 seconds. Stir in the onion and garlic and continue to cook for 2 minutes.

3 Add the celery, beetroot and squid. Mix the white wine and tomato purée and pour over the squid. Cover and cook on full for 8 minutes, or until the squid is tender.

4 Season with salt and pepper, and serve garnished with celery leaves.

COOK'S TIP

Squid with Beetroot is delicious served with buttered pasta. Small or medium-sized shells or short-cut macaroni are both suitable.

Alternatively, ladle the squid over a bed of cooked rice mixed with a little chopped parsley and freshly ground black pepper.

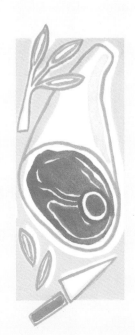

Meat and Poultry

Most poultry cooks very well in the microwave to give moist, flavoursome results in the minimum of time.
● Meat on chicken, turkey and duck is tender and needs short cooking.
● Duck is fatty so it does need to be crisped up before serving by placing under a hot grill or in a very hot oven.

The same rules apply to poultry as to fish when it comes to basic cooking.
● Arrange thick parts to the outside of the dish, cover the dish and do not sprinkle salt directly onto the poultry as it results in dry spots. Herbs, a knob of butter and plenty of black pepper are ideal flavour ingredients.
● If you like crisp skin, then brown it under the grill before serving. If you prefer, remove the skin before cooking for low-fat results.

Meat gives various results in the microwave.
● Tough cuts are not at their best cooked by this method.
● Braising steak can be cooked on medium or low to give acceptable results, but if you like your casseroles to 'melt-in-the-mouth', stick to conventional methods.
● Mince dishes are excellent as are those recipes which call for tender steak, lean pork and tender lamb.
● For plain cooked meat you may like to use a browning dish. To speed up the conventional roasting time for a large joint, part cook it in the microwave, then finish the roasting in the conventional oven for delicious, traditional results in extra quick time.

Use the following charts as a guide for defrosting and cooking fresh and frozen meat and poultry.

Fresh Meat and Poultry Cooking Guide

MEAT OR POULTRY	MINUTES ON FULL PER 450 G/1 LB, UNLESS OTHERWISE STATED	STANDING MINUTES
bacon joint	12–14	10
bacon, 4 rashers	4½	–
beef, boned joint, rare	5–6	15–20
beef, boned joint, medium	7–8	15–20
beef, boned joint, well-done	8–9	15–20
beef, joint with bone, rare	5–6	15–20
beef, joint with bone, medium	6–7	15–20
beef, joint with bone, well-done	8–9	15–20
beef, minced, 4 patties	10	5
chicken, whole	8–10	10–15
chicken, portions	6–8	10
lamb, boned joint	7–8	20
lamb, boned and rolled joint	9	20
lamb, joint with bone	6–7	20
lamb, crown roast	9–10	20
lamb chops	2	10
liver, ox	8	5
liver, lamb's, calves'	7	5
pork, boned rolled joint	8–10	15
pork, joint with bone	8–9	15
poussin, pigeon, pheasant, quail	5–7	5
sausages, 4	4	–
turkey, whole roast	11	10–15

Madras Beef Curry

SERVES 4

POWER SETTINGS: FULL AND MEDIUM

2 large onions

6 tbsp vegetable oil

4 sticks celery, chopped

675 g/1½ lb braising steak, cut into small cubes

1 tbsp flour

½ tsp paprika

½ tsp garam masala

1–2 tbsp Madras curry powder

1 tsp tomato purée

600 ml/1 pt boiling beef stock or water

1 (425-g/15-oz) can tomatoes

1 medium potato, diced

1 bay leaf

GARNISH

tomato slices

green chilli rings

lemon slices

parsley sprigs

1 Cut off a few thin onion rings for garnish, and then finely chop the remainder and place in a large casserole dish with the oil. Cook on full for 5 minutes.

2 Add the celery to the onions, stir well and continue to cook for a further 5 minutes.

3 Add the steak, flour, paprika and garam masala with the curry powder. Cover and cook on full for 5 minutes, stirring once. Add the tomato purée, stock and tomatoes, stirring thoroughly.

4 Cook the potato, covered, in a small basin on full for 5 minutes. Add to the curry with the bay leaf. Cook on medium for 40–45 minutes, until the meat is cooked and tender.

5 Serve the curry on a bed of cooked rice, garnished with the reserved onion, tomato slices, green chilli rings, lemon slices and parsley sprigs. Crisp popadoms complement the curry.

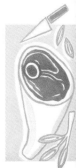

Frozen Meat and Poultry Defrosting Guide

MEAT OR POULTRY	MINUTES ON FULL PER 450 G/1 LB, UNLESS OTHERWISE STATED	STANDING MINUTES
beef, boned joint	8–10	30
beef, joint with bone	8–10	30
beef, minced	8–10	2
beef steak, cubed	6–8	5
hamburgers, 2	2	2
hamburgers, 4	4	2
chicken, whole	6–8	30
chicken portions	5	30
duck and duckling	5–7	30
kidney	6–9	5
lamb, boned joint	5–6	30–45
lamb, joint with bone	8–10	30–45
lamb chops	8–10	15
liver	8–10	5
pork, boned joint	7–8	30
pork, joint with bone	7–8	45
poussin, grouse, pigeon, pheasant	5–7	10
sausages	5–6	5
turkey, whole	10–12	60
veal, boned rolled joint	5–6	30
veal, joint with bone	8–10	45
veal chops	8–10	30
veal, minced	8–10	5

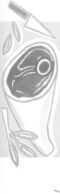

Thai Beef with Spinach

SERVES 4

POWER SETTINGS: FULL AND MEDIUM

300 ml/½ pt coconut milk (see Cook's Tip, below)

1 tsp brown sugar

1 tbsp mixed chopped nuts

1 tbsp soy sauce

675 g/1½ lb frying steak, cut into thin strips

2 cloves garlic, crushed

1 onion

2.5-cm/1-in piece fresh root ginger

2 chillies, seeded

salt and freshly ground black pepper

juice of ½ lemon

1 tbsp cornflour

450 g/1 lb frozen spinach or 1 kg/2 lb fresh spinach,
washed and trimmed

4 tbsp natural yogurt

GARNISH

chopped parsley

1 lemon slice

1 Put the coconut milk, sugar, nuts and soy sauce in a casserole dish and heat for 4 minutes on full. Mix the beef with these ingredients and cook on full for a further 7 minutes, stirring once.

2 In a blender or food processor make a paste with the garlic, onion, fresh ginger, chilli, a little salt and lemon juice. Mix this paste with the cornflour and a little cold water. Add some of the hot liquid from the beef to the mixture before stirring it into the casserole.

3 Cover and cook on medium for 25 minutes until the meat is cooked. Taste and season as necessary.

4 Place the frozen spinach in a bowl. Cover and cook on full for 12–15 minutes. Allow about 7–10 minutes for fresh spinach.

5 Drain the spinach thoroughly and place it on a warmed serving plate. Top with the beef and pour the yogurt over. Garnish with lemon and parsley. Serve at once.

COOK'S TIP

To make coconut milk, soak grated fresh coconut or desiccated coconut in boiling water to cover for 30 minutes. Drain and squeeze out all the liquid. The fresh coconut can be soaked for a second time to yield 'thin' coconut milk. Alternatively buy a block of creamed coconut and dissolve it in hot water.

Créole Steak

SERVES 4

POWER SETTING: FULL

4 fillet steaks (about 200 g/7 oz each)

50 g/2 oz butter, diced

2 onions, finely chopped

4 sticks celery, sliced

100 g/4 oz button mushrooms, chopped

1 (400-g/14-oz) can chopped tomatoes

2 tbsp tomato purée

1 tbsp soy sauce

salt and freshly ground black pepper

chopped parsley to garnish

1 Place the steaks in a casserole dish. Cook on full, uncovered, for 3–4 minutes depending on how well cooked you like your steak. Turn over and rearrange the steaks halfway through the cooking time.

2 Place the butter, onions, celery and mushrooms in a dish, cover and cook for 6 minutes, stirring after 3 minutes.

3 Stir in the remaining ingredients, season to taste, cover and cook on full for 4 minutes.

4 Arrange the steaks on a warmed serving dish. Pour the sauce over and sprinkle with parsley.

Beef Goulash

SERVES 4

POWER SETTINGS: FULL AND MEDIUM

1 kg/2 lb lean braising steak, cubed

50 g/2 oz plain flour

1½ tsp paprika

2 tbsp oil

2 cloves garlic, crushed

1 tbsp tomato purée

2 onions, sliced

600 ml/1 pt boiling beef stock

1 bay leaf

1 (200-g/7-oz) can tomatoes, mashed with their juice

4 tbsp natural yogurt

chopped parsley to garnish

1 Toss the meat in the flour and paprika.

2 Heat a browning dish according to the manufacturer's instructions. Pour the oil into the dish and cook on full for 1 minute. Add the meat and cook on full for 5 minutes, turning the cubes frequently to brown all sides.

Beef Goulash

3 Place the meat in a casserole with the garlic, tomato puree, onions, stock, bay leaf and tomatoes. Cover and cook on medium for 45 minutes, or until the beef is tender. Leave to stand for 5 minutes.

4 Spoon the yogurt over the goulash and serve garnished with parsley. The goulash goes well with buttered noodles or mashed potatoes.

Créole Steak

Beef Stroganoff

SERVES 4

POWER SETTING: FULL

25 g/1 oz butter

2 tbsp vegetable oil

350 g/12 oz fillet or rump steak, cut into thin 5-cm/2-in strips

1 small onion, finely chopped

1 tbsp flour

¼ tsp paprika

salt and freshly ground black pepper

1 tbsp brandy

2 tbsp Madeira or sherry

150 ml/¼ pt boiling beef stock

225 g/8 oz mushrooms, wiped and sliced

4 tbsp soured cream

GARNISH

chopped parsley

parsley sprigs

a few whole mushrooms, caps scored into spirals

1 Heat a browning dish according to the manufacturer's instructions.

2 Add the butter, oil and steak. Stir to brown the pieces, then add the onion. Cover and cook on full for 2 minutes.

3 Stir in the flour with the paprika and seasoning and coat the meat strips evenly.

4 In a mug or small basin, warm the brandy on full for 30 seconds. Pour over the meat and ignite.

VARIATIONS

Lamb Stroganoff: Substitute lamb fillet for the steak used in the above recipe. Prepare and cook the stroganoff as above and sprinkle with finely chopped tarragon or rosemary instead of parsley.

Pork Stroganoff: Substitute lean boneless pork for the steak. Prepare and cook the stroganoff as above.

Liver Stroganoff: Use lamb's liver instead of the steak. Carefully remove the thin membrane from the liver, then slice it and cut the slices into strips. Continue as above.

5 When the flames have died, add the Madeira or sherry, stir well. Gradually add the stock, stirring, then add the mushrooms to the sauce and cook on full for 4–5 minutes or until the sauce is thickened. Stir once during cooking to ensure that the meat cooks evenly.

6 Swirl the cream into the Stroganoff and serve it on a bed of cooked rice. Sprinkle with parsley and garnish with parsley sprigs. If you like add the whole mushrooms for garnish, cooking them with a knob of butter in a small basin on full for 1 minute first.

Spicy Meatloaf with Tomato Sauce

SERVES 4–6

POWER SETTING: FULL

1 tbsp oil

1 onion, chopped

1 clove garlic, chopped

225 g/8 oz minced beef

100 g/4 oz sausagemeat

100 g/4 oz bacon, rind removed and minced

50 g/2 oz fresh breadcrumbs

½ tsp ground mixed spice

1 tsp dried thyme

salt and freshly ground black pepper

1 egg, beaten

3 bay leaves

SAUCE

25 g/1 oz butter

1 onion, chopped

1 clove garlic, chopped

1 (425-g/15-oz) can tomatoes

1 tbsp tomato purée

1 tsp dried mixed herbs

salad ingredients to garnish

1 Mix the oil, onion and garlic in a bowl and cook on full for 3 minutes.

2 Add the beef, sausagemeat, bacon, breadcrumbs, spice, thyme and seasoning and mix well. Bind together with the beaten egg.

3 Press the mixture into a deep pie dish, top with the bay leaves. Cover and cook on full for 6 minutes. Wrap the loaf and dish in foil and leave to stand for 10–15 minutes. Remove the foil and cook for a further 5 minutes. Keep hot.

4 To make the sauce, place the butter, onion and garlic in a bowl and cook on full for 3 minutes. Add the remaining ingredients and seasoning to taste, then cook for a further 4 minutes. Blend the sauce in a blender or food processor and serve poured over the turned-out meatloaf, serve any extra separately. Garnish with salad ingredients.

Spicy Meatloaf with Tomato Sauce

Orange Lamb Chops

SERVES 4
POWER SETTING: FULL
8 lamb chops
1 tsp ground cinnamon
juice of 2 oranges
150 ml/¼ pt natural yogurt
1 egg yolk
salt and freshly ground black pepper

1 Heat a browning dish on full according to the manufacturer's instructions.

2 Add the chops and turn them almost immediately to brown both sides. Cook on full for 5 minutes, then rearrange the chops.

3 Add the cinnamon and orange juice. Cover and cook on full for 10–15 minutes, rearranging the chops once or twice, until they are cooked. Transfer the chops to a serving dish.

4 Mix the yogurt with the egg yolk. Add the yogurt mixture to the juices in the dish and season

to taste. Heat on full for 1–2 minutes, then pour the sauce over the chops and serve. Alternatively, the chops can be returned to the browning dish and served in the sauce.

Shepherd's Pie

SERVES 4
POWER SETTING: FULL
1 onion, chopped
2 tomatoes, peeled and chopped
2 carrots, chopped
1 clove garlic, chopped
300 ml/½ pt boiling beef or chicken stock
1 tbsp tomato purée
1 tbsp Worcestershire sauce
1 bay leaf
1 tsp dried mixed herbs
salt and freshly ground black pepper
1 tbsp fresh breadcrumbs
350 g/12 oz cooked beef or lamb, minced
675 g/1½ lb potatoes, cooked
25 g/1 oz butter
1 egg, beaten
parsley sprigs to garnish

1 Place the raw vegetables and garlic in a large pie dish with the stock. Cover and cook on full for 5 minutes.

2 Stir in the tomato purée, Worcestershire sauce, herbs, seasoning, breadcrumbs and meat.

3 Mash the cooked potatoes with the butter and beaten egg and spread over the meat. Cook on full for 15 minutes, then brown under the grill before serving, garnished with parsley.

Shepherd's Pie

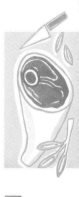

Veal with Cream and Mushroom Sauce

SERVES 4

POWER SETTING: FULL

450 g/1 lb veal fillet, trimmed and diced

25 g/1 oz plain flour

salt and freshly ground black pepper

50 g/2 oz butter

1 onion, chopped

100 g/4 oz button mushrooms

300 ml/½ pt dry white wine

300 ml/½ pt boiling chicken stock

1 tsp lemon juice

1 tsp dried sage

1 tbsp single cream

1 egg yolk

GARNISH

crispy bacon rolls

puff pastry crescents

1 Toss the veal in the flour and a little seasoning. Place the butter in a large dish and cook on full for 1 minute. Stir in the veal and cook on full for 6 minutes, stirring once.

2 Remove veal and set aside. Place the onion and mushrooms in the dish, then cook on full for 3 minutes.

3 Stir in the veal, wine, stock, lemon juice and sage, and cook, covered, for 20 minutes, stirring once.

4 Stir in the cream and egg yolk and serve garnished with crispy bacon rolls and puff pastry crescents.

MICROWAVE TIP	
Bacon rolls can be cooked in the microwave: de-rind the bacon, roll the rashers and secure them with wooden cocktail sticks.	Place the rolls on a plate or microwave roasting rack and cover with absorbent kitchen paper, cook on full, allow 5–7 minutes for eight rolls.

Crown Roast of Lamb with Apricot Rice Stuffing

SERVES 6–8

POWER SETTING: FULL

1 crown roast prepared from 2 best ends of neck of lamb

1 tbsp soy sauce

1 tbsp oil

salt and freshly ground black pepper

25 g/1 oz butter

1 onion, finely chopped

2 sticks celery, chopped

100 g/4 oz long-grain rice, cooked

1 (425-g/15-oz) can apricots, drained and chopped

1 tbsp sultanas

1 tbsp chopped mixed nuts

1 egg, beaten

1 tbsp chopped parsley

GARNISH

1 (425-g/15-oz) can apricot halves, drained

parsley sprigs

1 Make sure that the crown roast is as lean as possible and trim any visible fat from the inside. Brush the outside with soy sauce and oil. Sprinkle the inside with seasoning.

2 Place the butter, onion and celery in a basin. Cover and cook on full for 5 minutes. Add all the remaining ingredients and mix well. Reserve a little of this stuffing to fill the apricot halves for garnish and use the rest to fill the crown roast. Weigh the joint.

3 Stand the meat in a dish. Cover the tips of the bones with small pieces of foil to prevent them

overcooking. Calculate the cooking time at 5–6 minutes per 450 g/1 lb. Place a large roasting bag over the joint and cook on full for a quarter of the calculated time. Leave to stand for 15 minutes, cook for a second quarter of the time and leave to stand for another 15 minutes. Cook for the remaining time, then leave the joint to stand for 15 minutes, tented with foil (shiny side inwards), before serving.

4 While the joint is cooking, fill the apricot halves for garnishing with the reserved stuffing. Place in a dish. Pour a little of the cooking juices from the meat over the stuffing, then cook on full for 4–5 minutes while the joint is standing.

5 Serve the joint garnished with parsley sprigs and the apricots filled with stuffing.

Crown Roast of Lamb with Apricot Rice Stuffing

Moussaka

SERVES 4

POWER SETTING: FULL

1 large aubergine, trimmed and sliced

salt

25 g/1 oz butter

2 onions, chopped

2 cloves garlic, chopped

100 g/4 oz mushrooms, sliced

450 g/1 lb minced lamb

2 tbsp tomato purée

1 tsp dried mixed herbs

150 ml/¼ pt boiling beef stock

SAUCE

25 g/1 oz butter

25 g/1 oz plain flour

300 ml/½ pt milk

50 g/2 oz Edam cheese, grated

1 egg, beaten

generous pinch of grated nutmeg

1 Sprinkle the aubergine slices with salt and leave to degorge for 30 minutes. Rinse in cold water and pat dry with absorbent kitchen paper.

2 Place the aubergine slices in a bowl, cover and cook on full for 3 minutes. Set aside.

3 Place the butter, onions, garlic and mushrooms in a bowl. Cover and cook on full for 3 minutes. Stir in the meat, tomato purée, herbs and stock. Cover and cook on full for 15 minutes.

4 For the sauce, place the butter in a bowl and cook on full for 1 minute. Stir in the flour, then gradually add the milk and cook on full for 3 minutes, stirring once. Stir in the cheese, egg and nutmeg.

5 Layer the lamb mixture and aubergine slices alternately in a casserole. Pour the sauce over the top and cook on full for 10 minutes, turning the dish once. Allow to stand for 5 minutes before serving. Crusty bread and a green salad are ideal accompaniments.

Chilled Noisettes of Lamb with Cranberry Glaze

SERVES 2

POWER SETTING: FULL

4 noisettes of lamb (about 75 g/3 oz each)

1 (400-g/14-oz) can consommé

1 tbsp gelatine

6 tbsp cranberry sauce

1 tsp chopped fresh mint or ½ tsp dried mint

salad ingredients to garnish

1 Arrange the noisettes in a shallow dish. Cook on full for 2 minutes, rearrange, then cook for a further 2 minutes. Set aside to cool, placing the lamb on absorbent kitchen paper to remove all excess fat.

2 Pour the consommé into a bowl and cook on full for 3 minutes, or until heated but not boiling. Sprinkle the gelatine over, leave to soften for 2 minutes, then stir until the gelatine has dissolved completely. If necessary heat the consommé on full for 15–30 seconds.

3 Heat the cranberry sauce on full for 1 minute, then stir well. Stir half the consommé into the cranberry sauce and leave until just beginning to set. Chill the remaining consommé until set.

4 Arrange the lamb on a serving plate and coat with the cranberry sauce. Chill until set. Chop the consommé and arrange it on the plate with the lamb. Garnish with salad ingredients.

Transylvanian Goulash

SERVES 4

POWER SETTINGS: FULL AND MEDIUM

1 tbsp oil

1 large onion, finely chopped

2 tbsp paprika

675 g/1½ lb lean boneless pork, cubed

1 large clove garlic, crushed

2 tsp dried dill

2 tsp caraway seeds

300 ml/½ pt boiling water

675 g/1½ lb sauerkraut

salt and freshly ground black pepper

150 ml/¼ pt soured cream

1 Mix the oil and onion in a casserole dish and cook on full for 4 minutes.

2 Add the paprika and stir well. Add the pork, garlic, dill and caraway seeds. Stir well, then cook on full for 4 minutes, stirring once.

3 Pour in the water and stir in the sauerkraut, then cook on full for 10 minutes. Stir well, add seasoning and continue to cook on medium for 15–20 minutes. Stir in the soured cream and cook on full for 1 minute before serving.

Pork in Cider

SERVES 4

POWER SETTING: FULL

4 slices pork fillet

300 ml/½ pt dry cider

juice of ½ lemon

1 tbsp chopped mixed fresh herbs

3 tbsp oil

1 carrot, sliced

1 onion, sliced

2 courgettes, sliced

1 cooking apple, cored and sliced

1 chicken stock cube

1 tsp cornflour

2 tbsp water

salt and freshly ground black pepper

chopped parsley to garnish

1 Marinate the pork in the cider, lemon juice and herbs for 30 minutes.

2 Pour the oil into a large shallow casserole and cook on full for 1 minute. Stir in the vegetables and apple, and cook for a further 3 minutes.

3 Add the pork with its marinade and cook on full for 6 minutes, stirring once. Crumble in the chicken stock cube. Blend the cornflour to a paste with the water, add to the casserole and season well. Cover and cook on full for 15 minutes. Allow to stand for 5 minutes, rearrange the meat and cook for a further 5 minutes or until the pork is cooked. Sprinkle with parsley and serve.

COOK'S TIP

Pipe a ring of mashed potato in a gratin dish, brown the top under a hot grill and serve the pork in cider in the middle. Alternatively, serve the pork with buttered green tagliatelle or wholewheat spaghetti.

Top: Transylvanian Goulash; Bottom: Pork in Cider

Pork Kebabs

SERVES 4

POWER SETTING: FULL

575 g/1¼ lb lean boneless pork, cubed

juice of 2 lemons

3 tbsp olive oil

salt and freshly ground black pepper

1 tsp dried oregano

1 small aubergine, trimmed and cubed

1 small green pepper, seeded and cubed

1 small red pepper, seeded and cubed

1 Place the pork in a bowl with the lemon juice, oil, salt, pepper and oregano and marinate for 2 hours. Add the vegetables and toss them in the marinade.

2 Thread the ingredients onto eight wooden skewers. Place the kebabs in a shallow dish and brush with the marinade, then cook on full for 11 minutes, turning and basting frequently. Serve with rice and a green salad.

MICROWAVE TIP

The most tender cuts of meat cook best in the microwave. Any cut of pork is suitable if it is	well trimmed, but the fillet will give the best results.

Pork Spare Ribs in Barbecue Sauce

SERVES 2

POWER SETTINGS: FULL AND LOW

15 g/½ oz butter

1 small onion, finely sliced

6 meaty pork spare ribs (about 675 g/1½ lb total weight)

BARBECUE SAUCE

2 tbsp clear honey

2 tbsp soy sauce

4 tbsp tomato ketchup

1 tbsp white wine vinegar

salad ingredients to garnish

1 Place the butter and onion in a shallow casserole. Cover and cook on full for 3 minutes.

Sweet and Sour Spare Rib Chops

SERVES 4
POWER SETTING: FULL
675 g/1½ lb spare rib chops
25 g/1 oz butter
1 small onion, chopped
25 g/1 oz red or green pepper, chopped
25 g/1 oz carrot, chopped
4 cloves garlic, chopped
4 thin slices fresh root ginger, chopped
25 g/1 oz cornflour
1 tbsp tomato ketchup
25 g/1 oz brown sugar
1 tbsp sherry
3 tbsp red wine vinegar
1 tbsp soy sauce
salt
green pepper rings to garnish

2 Add the ribs to the casserole dish. In a small bowl mix the honey, soy sauce, ketchup and wine vinegar. Cook on full for 1 minute, stir well and pour over the pork, coating the ribs evenly. Cook on full for 4 minutes.

3 Spoon the sauce over the ribs, cover and cook on low for 25 minutes, rearranging and turning the ribs every 5 minutes.

4 Use a slotted spoon to transfer the ribs to a warmed serving dish and keep hot. Replace the dish of sauce in the microwave and cook on full for about 4–5 minutes, or until bubbling hot. Coat the ribs in sauce and garnish with salad.

1 Place the chops in a large shallow dish and cook on full for 5 minutes. Remove from the dish and set aside.

2 Add the butter, onion, pepper, carrot, garlic and ginger to the juices and cook on full for 3 minutes. Stir in the cornflour, then gradually stir in all the remaining ingredients.

3 Add the chops to the sauce, turning them to coat them completely. Cover and cook on full for 18 minutes, turning the chops and stirring the sauce once. Leave to stand for 5 minutes before serving, garnished with green pepper rings. Plain cooked rice makes a good accompaniment

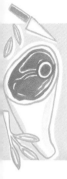

Glazed Ham with Apricots

Glazed Ham with Apricots

SERVES 6

POWER SETTING: FULL

1 ham joint, weighing about 3 kg/6 lb, soaked overnight

1 (425-g/15-oz) can apricots

3 tbsp clear honey

100 g/4 oz brown sugar

about 6 cloves

1 If you like, remove the skin from the joint. Score the fat (or the skin if left on) into a diamond pattern, then tie the joint securely in shape with string. Place the ham, best side down, on an inverted plate, or microwave roasting rack, in a shallow dish and cover with greased waxed paper. Alternatively, place both the ham and the dish in a large roasting bag. Calculate the cooking time, allowing 12–14 minutes per 450 g/1 lb. Cook on full for half the time, then set aside for 30 minutes.

2 Drain the apricots and pour the juice into a bowl. Add the honey and cook on full for 3 minutes. Brush the ham with this syrup, sprinkle with half the sugar and stick with cloves. Turn and cook on full for the remaining time.

3 Add the remaining sugar to the syrup and cook on full for 3 minutes, stirring once. Glaze the ham, cool and garnish with apricot halves.

Liver in Port and Orange Sauce

SERVES 4

POWER SETTING: FULL

100 g/4 oz butter

1 clove garlic, chopped

4 tbsp orange juice

2 tbsp chopped parsley

675 g/1½ lb lamb's or calf's liver, sliced

2 tsp cornflour

4 tbsp port

grated rind of 1 orange

salt and freshly ground black pepper

1 Place the butter, garlic, orange juice and parsley in a bowl. Cover and cook on full for 3 minutes.

2 Add the liver slices, making sure they are well coated in the sauce. Cover and cook on full for 7–10 minutes, or until the liver is almost cooked.

3 Blend the cornflour with the port and orange rind and stir it into the liver. Cook, uncovered, on full for 2 minutes, rearranging once. Taste and adjust the seasoning. Serve with mashed potato and a green vegetable, such as spinach or broccoli.

Lamb's Liver with Creamy Tomato Sauce

SERVES 4

POWER SETTING: FULL

25 g/1 oz butter

2–3 tbsp oil

1 large onion, sliced

1 clove garlic, crushed (optional)

450 g/1 lb lamb's liver, sliced

2–3 tbsp sherry

150 ml/¼ pt boiling stock

1 (200-g/7-oz) can peeled tomatoes

salt and freshly ground black pepper

3 tbsp whipping cream

GARNISH

1 tbsp freshly chopped parsley

parsley sprigs

tomato wedges

1 Place the butter, oil, onion and garlic (if used) in a casserole and cook on full for 4 minutes. Add the liver, turning the pieces to coat them in the fat.

2 Add the sherry, stock and tomatoes. Cover and cook on full for 8–10 minutes, rearranging the liver slices twice to ensure that they cook evenly.

3 Taste and adjust the seasoning, then stir in the cream and heat for 30 seconds on full.

4 Serve on a bed of cooked rice, topped with chopped parsley and garnished with parsley sprigs and tomato wedges.

Sage and Mozzarella-stuffed Chicken

SERVES 6

POWER SETTING: FULL

1.5–2 kg/3.5–4 lb oven-ready chicken, body cavity scalded

6 sage leaves

25–50 g/1–2 oz mozzarella cheese, sliced

25 g/1 oz butter

1 onion, chopped

50 g/2 oz fresh white breadcrumbs

2 tsp chopped fresh sage

salt and freshly ground black pepper

150 ml/¼ pt boiling chicken stock

25 g/1 oz butter

1 tbsp brown sugar

1 tbsp sherry

sage leaves to garnish

1 Grasp the flap of skin at the end of the bird and with the other hand, pull the skin away from the flesh as far as you can. Slide in sage leaves and cheese slices under the skin.

2 Place the butter and onion in a bowl, cover and cook on full for 3 minutes. Add the breadcrumbs, sage, seasoning and stock to form a moist stuffing. Spoon this into the body cavity of the chicken.

3 Weigh the bird and calculate the cooking time at 8–10 minutes per 450 g/1 lb. Cook on full for half the calculated time. Place the butter, sugar and sherry in a small bowl. Cook on full for 1 minute. Brush the bird with this glaze, then cook for the remaining time. Check to see if the chicken is done by sticking a skewer into it where the leg joins with the breast. The juices should run clear of any signs of blood.

4 Allow to stand for 15 minutes before serving, garnished with sage.

Coq au Vin

SERVES 4

POWER SETTING: FULL

100 g/4 oz salt pork or unsmoked bacon, rind removed
and cut into pieces

1 tbsp flour

100 ml/4 oz boiling chicken stock

½ bottle red wine

small glass of brandy

1 tsp tomato purée

2 bay leaves

1 tsp dried thyme

salt and freshly ground black pepper

2 cloves garlic, crushed

15 button onions

175 g/6 oz button mushrooms

8 small chicken portions (thighs and drumsticks)
or 4 chicken quarters

GARNISH

fingers of toast and watercress sprigs

1 Place the salt pork or bacon in a casserole and cook on full for 4–5 minutes. Remove and reserve, then stir the flour into the dripping.

2 Gradually stir in the stock, wine and brandy, then add the tomato purée, bay leaves, thyme, salt and pepper. Stir in the garlic, onions and mushrooms. Cover and cook on full for 12 minutes or until the sauce is just boiling.

3 Stir in the pork or bacon and arrange the chicken in the sauce. Cook, uncovered for 12 minutes or until chicken is cooked. Turn and rearrange the portions halfway through cooking. Allow to stand for 10 minutes before serving, garnished with fingers of toast and watercress.

Tandoori Chicken

SERVES 4

POWER SETTINGS: FULL AND MEDIUM

4 chicken leg portions (about 225 g/8 oz each)

3 tbsp tandoori paste

150 ml/¼ pt natural yogurt

GARNISH

onion rings

lemon slices

1 Skin the chicken portions and make three or four deep slashes into the flesh. Place in a dish.

2 Mix the tandoori paste and yogurt, pour the mixture over the chicken and marinate for at least 2 hours.

3 Remove the chicken from the marinade, place on a microwave roasting rack, cover and cook on full for 10 minutes, turning halfway through the cooking time.

4 Cook on medium for a further 15–17 minutes, turning and rearranging twice. When cooked, the juices from the chicken should run clear. If they are pink, cook a little longer, checking regularly by piercing the meat at the thickest part.

5 If you like, brown the chicken under a hot grill before serving, garnished with onion rings and lemon slices. Serve with salad and yellow rice.

Turkey Escalopes with White Wine and Mushroom Sauce

SERVES 4
POWER SETTING: FULL
4 turkey breast fillets (about 450 g/1 lb total weight), beaten thin
¼ tsp paprika
50 g/2 oz butter
2 tbsp vegetable oil
1 onion
100 g/4 oz mushrooms, wiped and sliced
2–3 tbsp white wine
300 ml/½ pt milk
1 bouquet garni
1 bay leaf
4 peppercorns, lightly crushed
20 g/¾ oz plain flour
salt and freshly ground black pepper
GARNISH
chopped spring onion
lemon twist
sprigs of parsley

1 Dust the turkey with the paprika. Heat a browning dish according to the manufacturer's instructions. Add half the butter, the oil and the turkey, turning the pieces in the hot dish to brown both sides of each escalope.

2 Cut a thick slice from the onion and set it aside for the sauce. Finely chop the remainder and sprinkle it over the turkey. Cover the dish and cook on full for 7–8 minutes, turning the turkey halfway through, until just cooked.

3 Add the mushrooms and wine and cook, covered, on full for a further 2 minutes.

4 Place the milk, reserved onion slice, bouquet garni, bay leaf and peppercorns in a microwave-proof jug. Heat on full for 3–4 minutes, until just boiling, then set aside to stand for 10 minutes.

5 Cream the remaining butter with the flour, then gradually stir in the strained milk. Cook on full for 4 minutes, until boiling and thickened, whisking thoroughly once during cooking and at the end of the cooking time.

6 Pour the sauce over the turkey and mix well to combine it with the cooking liquid. Cover and cook for 1–2 minutes, until thoroughly heated. Serve at once, on a bed of yellow rice. Garnish with chopped spring onion, lemon and parsley sprigs.

Duck in Orange Sauce

SERVES 4

POWER SETTINGS: MEDIUM AND FULL

4 duck portions

SAUCE

1 tbsp orange jelly marmalade

250 ml/8 fl oz fresh orange juice

2 tbsp port

2 tbsp lemon juice

2 tbsp clear honey

2 tsp cornflour

1 tbsp water

GARNISH

orange slices

watercress sprigs

1 Arrange the duck portions on a microwave roasting rack in a large dish. Cook, covered, on medium for 45–60 minutes. Rearrange and turn the duck portions several times during cooking and drain off the fat. Test to see that they are cooked by piercing with a sharp knife at the joint, the juices should run clear. Brown the cooked duck under a conventional grill.

2 For the sauce, place the jelly marmalade in a dish and cook on full for 1 minute. Add the remaining sauce ingredients, except the cornflour and water, and cook for a further 3 minutes or until bubbling.

3 Blend the cornflour to a paste with the water. Stir into the sauce and cook on full for 1 minute. Stir well.

4 Place the duck on a warm serving dish, pour over the sauce and garnish with orange slices and watercress.

Stuffed Poussins

SERVES 4

POWER SETTING: FULL

450 ml/¾ pt natural yogurt

1 tbsp cornflour

4 tbsp water

1½ tsp ground cumin

1½ tsp ground cinnamon

salt and freshly ground black pepper

4 poussins, with skin removed

100 g/4 oz long-grain rice, cooked

6 tbsp raisins

4 tbsp flaked almonds

1 First prepare the yogurt sauce, put the yogurt in a basin and mix the cornflour and the water. Stir into the yogurt and cook on full for 5–6 minutes or until boiling. Stir well halfway through cooking, then again at the end of the cooking time. Cook for a further 4 minutes.

2 Add the cumin, cinnamon, salt and pepper. Set aside while you stuff the poussins.

3 Mix the rice, raisins, almonds, salt and pepper together, and stuff the mixture inside the poussins. Tie the legs together with string or thread. Place the poussins breasts down in a dish. Spoon over the prepared yogurt mixture and cover.

4 Cook on full for 10 minutes, then turn the birds over and cook for a further 15–18 minutes. The exact cooking time will depend on the size of the poussins. Brown the birds for a few minutes under a hot grill and serve at once, with the sauce poured over.

Vegetables

You are probably aware – or you will certainly have heard – that the microwave cooks vegetables well. A few points ensure success.

● Cook the vegetables with a little water and cover the dish or put the vegetables in a roasting bag.

● Do not salt the vegetables before cooking as this results in dry spots on the cooked food.

One of the great advantages of the microwave cooker is that foods can be partly cooked, then left covered to be cooked completely just before serving. This is helpful when planning dinner parties – have the part-cooked vegetables in suitable serving dishes ready to be put in the microwave for a few minutes while everyone enjoys the first course.

The following charts offer a guide to cooking times for both frozen and fresh vegetables.

Fresh Vegetables Cooking Guide

VEGETABLES	QUANTITY	MINUTES ON FULL
artichokes, globe	4	10–20
asparagus spears	225 g/8 oz	6–7
aubergines, diced	450 g/1 lb	5–6
beans, broad, French or runner	450 g/1 lb	8–10
beetroot, sliced	450 g/1 lb	7–8
broccoli spears	450 g/1 lb	4–5
Brussels sprouts	450 g/1 lb	8–10
cabbage, shredded	450 g/1 lb	7–10
carrots, sliced	225 g/8 oz	7–10
cauliflower florets	450 g/1 lb	10–11
celery	1 head	10–13
corn-on-the-cob	1	3–5
courgettes, sliced	4	7–10
greens, chopped	450 g/1 lb	7–9
kohlrabi	450 g/1 lb	7–8
leeks, sliced	450 g/1 lb	7–10
marrow, sliced	450 g/1 lb	8–10
mushrooms, whole	225 g/8 oz	5–6
okra	225 g/8 oz	8–10
onions, sliced	225 g/8 oz	5–7
parsnips, sliced	225 g/8 oz	8–10
peas	450 g/1 lb	7
potatoes, new	450 g/1 lb	8–10
potatoes, baked in their jackets	2 large	8
potatoes, boiled	450 g/1 lb	6–7
spinach	450 g/1 lb	5
swedes, sliced	450 g/1 lb	6–7
tomatoes, sliced	450 g/1 lb	2–3
turnips, sliced	225 g/8 oz	6–7

Frozen Vegetables Cooking Guide

VEGETABLES	QUANTITY	MINUTES ON FULL
asparagus spears	225 g/8 oz	6–7
beans, broad, French or runner	225 g/8 oz	7
broccoli spears	225 g/8 oz	6–8
cabbage, chopped	225 g/8 oz	6–7
carrots, sliced	225 g/8 oz	6–7
cauliflower florets	225 g/8 oz	4–6
corn-on-the-cob	1	4–5
courgettes, sliced	225 g/8 oz	4
peas	225 g/8 oz	4
spinach, chopped	225 g/8 oz	5
sweet corn	225 g/8 oz	4–6
swedes, cubed	225 g/8 oz	7
turnips, sliced	225 g/8 oz	8
vegetables, mixed	225 g/8 oz	4–6

Baked Potatoes with Soured Cream and Chives

SERVES 1

POWER SETTING: FULL

1 (275-g/10-oz) potato, scrubbed

2 tbsp soured cream

1 tsp snipped chives

salt and freshly ground black pepper

crispy bacon bits to garnish

1 Prick the potato and place it on a double-thick piece of absorbent kitchen paper directly on the turntable or floor of the oven. Cook on full for about 7–9 minutes, or until tender.

2 Cut the potato in half. Scoop out a spoonful of potato and mix it with the soured cream, chives and seasoning to taste. Spoon this mixture back into the potato, top with crispy bacon bits and cook on full for 1 minute before serving.

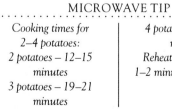

MICROWAVE TIP

Cooking times for 2–4 potatoes:	4 potatoes – 26–30 minutes
2 potatoes – 12–15 minutes	Reheat filling for just 1–2 minutes in all cases.
3 potatoes – 19–21 minutes	

Hot Oatmeal Potatoes

SERVES 4

POWER SETTING: FULL

1 kg/2 lb new potatoes, scrubbed

4 tbsp water

50 g/2 oz butter

6 spring onions, chopped

75 g/3 oz porridge oats

1 tbsp chopped parsley

1 Prick the new potatoes several times with a fork. Place in a deep dish with water. Cover and cook on full for 10 minutes or until tender. Allow to stand for 3 minutes. Drain and slice.

2 Melt the butter in a dish on full for 1 minute. Add most of the spring onions, stir well, and mix in the sliced potatoes and the oatmeal. Cook on full for 5 minutes.

3 Sprinkle with the remaining chopped spring onion and the parsley. Serve at once.

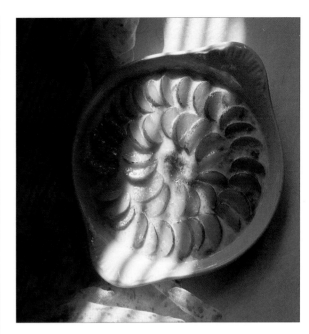

Dauphinois Potatoes

SERVES 4

POWER SETTING: FULL

1 kg/2 lb small new potatoes

4 tbsp water

300 ml/½ pt milk

1 bay leaf

2 parsley sprigs

1 slice onion

salt and freshly ground white pepper

25 g/1 oz butter

1 clove garlic, crushed

250 ml/8 fl oz double cream

1 Prick the new potatoes with a fork, place in a dish with the water and cook on full for 10 minutes or until tender. Allow to stand for 3 minutes.

2 Drain and slice the potatoes thinly.

3 Heat the milk with the bay leaf, parsley, onion slice and seasoning. Generously butter a dish with the butter mixed with the garlic and arrange the sliced potatoes in it.

4 Strain over the hot milk, then cook, uncovered, on full for 10 minutes. Season the potatoes well and pour in the cream. Cook on full for 3 minutes, then allow to stand for 3 minutes.

5 Lightly brown the potatoes under a hot grill and serve at once.

Layered Leeks

Turnip and Potato Bake

SERVES 4

POWER SETTING: FULL

450 g/1 lb turnips, thinly sliced

450 g/1 lb potatoes, thinly sliced

50 g/2 oz butter

salt and freshly ground black pepper

4 tbsp single cream

snipped chives to garnish

1 Layer the turnips and potatoes in a round dish, dotting each layer with butter and seasoning with salt and pepper. Cover with waxed paper and press well down.

Buttered Carrots with Orange Sauce

2 Put a lid on the dish and cook on full for 9 minutes, turning once. Test to make sure that the vegetables are cooked by inserting the blade of a knife into the middle of them. If they still feel slightly raw, then cook for a further 1–2 minutes and test again.

3 Slowly pour the cream over the vegetables, so that it seeps between the layers. Brown the top under a hot grill and sprinkle with chives before serving.

Layered Leeks

SERVES 4

POWER SETTING: FULL

50 g/2 oz butter

2–3 potatoes, thinly sliced

2 parsnips, thinly sliced

1 onion, thinly sliced

salt and freshly ground black pepper

300 ml/½ pt milk

3 leeks, washed and sliced

¼ tsp grated nutmeg

50 ml/2 fl oz single cream

2 tbsp grated cheese

1 Use half the butter to generously grease a 1.4-L/2½-pt dish. Arrange half the potatoes and all of

Turnip and Potato Bake

the parsnips and onion in layers. Season each layer well and pour the milk over the top.

2 Cook on full for 5 minutes, then leave to stand for 2 minutes. Cook on full for a further 5 minutes.

3 Arrange the leeks on top of the other vegetables, season with nutmeg and top with the remaining potatoes. Pour the cream over the vegetables and dot with the remaining butter.

4 Cook for 10–12 minutes on full. Check to see if the vegetables are tender and cook for a further 2–3 minutes if necessary.

5 Sprinkle with cheese and brown under the grill, then serve at once.

Buttered Carrots with Orange

SERVES 4

POWER SETTING: FULL

400 g/14 oz carrots, cut into neat strips

40 g/1½ oz butter

2 tbsp orange juice

salt and white pepper

GARNISH

pared rind of ¼ orange, cut into thin strips

4 tbsp water

orange slices

1 Put the carrots in a dish with the butter and orange juice, cover and cook on full for about 10 minutes, until tender. Stir or shake the vegetables a couple of times during cooking.

2 For the garnish, place the strips of orange rind in a mug or small bowl with the water. Cook on full for 2 minutes, then drain.

3 Season the carrots with salt and white pepper to taste, then serve, garnished with the orange slices and rind.

Carrots with Yogurt

Beetroot in Onion Sauce

SERVES 4

POWER SETTING: FULL

25 g/1 oz butter

1 onion, chopped

1 clove garlic, crushed

600 ml/1 pt Béchamel Sauce (see page 111)

grated rind and juice of 1 lemon

½ tsp paprika

675 g/1½ lb cooked beetroot

50 ml/2 fl oz double cream (optional)

1 tbsp chopped parsley or snipped chives

1 In a bowl, melt the butter on full for 1 minute. Add the onion and garlic and continue to cook for 3 minutes or until the onion is transparent.

2 Season the Béchamel sauce well and add the lemon rind and paprika.

3 Add the beetroot to the onion mixture and sprinkle with lemon juice. Cook, covered, for 5 minutes. Pour the Béchamel sauce over.

4 Drizzle the cream (if used) over the beetroot and sprinkle with parsley or chives. Serve at once.

MICROWAVE TIP

To cook raw beetroot in the microwave, place the whole vegetables in a large bowl with about 150 ml/¼ pt water.

Cover and cook on full, allowing 15–20 minutes for 675 g/1½ lb. Rearrange halfway through cooking.

Caraway Cabbage

Beetroot in Onion Sauce

Caraway Cabbage

SERVES 4

POWER SETTING: FULL

675 g/1½ lb white or green cabbage, finely shredded

25 g/1 oz butter

1 tbsp caraway seeds

salt and fresh ground black pepper

150 ml/¼ pt soured cream

1 Place the cabbage in a bowl. Add the butter and cook on full for 2 minutes. Stir well, add the caraway seeds, cover and cook for a further 8–10 minutes or until the cabbage is cooked to your liking.

2 Season to taste, stir in the soured cream and cook on full for a further 2 minutes. Serve at once.

Carrots with Yogurt

SERVES 4

POWER SETTING: FULL

450 g/1 lb carrots, sliced

½ tsp sugar

4 tbsp water

½ tsp ground cumin

1 small onion, finely chopped

juice of ½ lemon

150 ml/¼ pt natural yogurt

salt and freshly ground black pepper

cumin seeds to garnish (optional)

1 Place the carrots and sugar in a bowl with the water and cook, covered, on full for about 12 minutes. Stir halfway through cooking.

2 Drain them and add the cumin and onion; stir. Mix the lemon juice into the yogurt, season to taste and spoon it over the carrots.

3 Serve immediately or leave it to cool and serve as a salad or an accompaniment to curry. Sprinkle with cumin seeds, if you like.

Striped Cabbage Casserole

Striped Cabbage Casserole

SERVES 4

POWER SETTING: FULL

25 g/1 oz butter

1 onion, chopped

1 parsnip, diced

2 carrots, diced

225 g/8 oz green cabbage, finely shredded

225 g/8 oz red cabbage, finely shredded

1 (425-g/15-oz) can tomatoes or 1 kg/2 lb fresh tomatoes, peeled

600 ml/1 pt boiling vegetable stock

1 tsp tomato purée

½ tsp soy sauce

salt and freshly ground black pepper

1 tsp dried mixed herbs

1 Place the butter and onion in a dish and cook on full for 1 minute.

2 Add the parsnip and carrots and cook on full for 1 minute. Stir and cook for another 2 minutes.

3 Reserve about a quarter of each colour of cabbage for the top of the casserole, and add the rest to the vegetables. Add the tomatoes, stock, tomato purée, soy sauce, seasoning and herbs, and mix well.

4 Cover and cook on full for 10 minutes. Remove and stir, tasting for seasoning. Arrange the remaining cabbage in alternate red and green stripes on top of the casserole. Return to the microwave and cook for a further 5 minutes on full. The cooked cabbage should be fairly crisp.

Broccoli and Cauliflower Cheese

SERVES 4

POWER SETTING: FULL

450 g/1 lb broccoli spears

4 tsp water

1 cauliflower, broken into florets

2 potatoes, thinly sliced

salt and freshly ground pepper

50 ml/2 fl oz milk

600 ml/1 pt Béchamel Sauce (see page 111)

4 slices cheese

1 tbsp browned breadcrumbs

1 Arrange the broccoli in a round dish with the heads facing in to the centre and stalks out. Add the water and cook, covered, on full for 5 minutes.

2 Arrange the cauliflower florets in the same way. Cook on full for 5 minutes, stand for 3 minutes.

Broccoli and Cauliflower Cheese

3 Arrange the potatoes on the bottom of a buttered deep dish. Season the milk, then pour it over the potatoes, partially cover and cook on full for 5 minutes, or until tender. Stand for 3 minutes.

4 Arrange the broccoli and cauliflower on top. Pour over the Béchamel Sauce and cook for 10 minutes on full.

5 Sprinkle with freshly ground pepper and top with the slices of cheese. Cook on full for 2 minutes or until the cheese has melted. Sprinkle with the breadcrumbs and brown the top under the grill, if liked. Allow to stand for 2 minutes, then serve while the cheese is still soft.

Red Cabbage and Apple

SERVES 4
POWER SETTING: FULL
450 g/1 lb red cabbage, finely shredded
225 g/8 oz cooking apples, peeled, cored and sliced
4 tbsp red wine vinegar
2 tbsp brown sugar
pinch of ground mixed spice
salt and freshly ground black pepper

1 Mix all the ingredients together in a large dish, tossing the cabbage and apple well to make sure they are coated in vinegar, sugar and seasoning.

2 Cover and cook on full for 15 minutes, stirring twice, until tender but still crunchy.

Red Cabbage and Apple

71

Creamed Spinach

SERVES 4
POWER SETTING: FULL
1 kg/2 lb fresh spinach
150 ml/¼ pt water
25 g/1 oz butter
25 g/1 oz plain flour
salt and freshly ground black pepper
freshly grated nutmeg
100 ml/4 fl oz cream

1 Prepare the spinach: remove the thick stalks and tear the leaves into strips. Place in a dish with the water. Cover and cook on full for 3 minutes. Drain thoroughly in a sieve, reserving the liquid.

2 Melt the butter in a dish on full for 1 minute. Add the flour and stir well. Pour in the liquid from the spinach, season and add nutmeg, then cook on full for 1 minute; remove and whisk briskly.

3 Beat in the cream and return the sauce to the microwave to cook for a further 1 minute on full. Remove and whisk again until smooth.

4 Add the cooked spinach and mix well. Reheat on full for 3 minutes or until heated through. Serve at once.

Spinach Roulade

SERVES 6
POWER SETTINGS: FULL AND MEDIUM
450 g/1 lb fresh spinach, washed and trimmed
15 g/½ oz butter
3 eggs, separated
grated nutmeg
salt and freshly ground black pepper
100 g/4 oz curd cheese
150 ml/¼ pt soured cream
4 spring onions, finely chopped

1 Line an oblong flan dish measuring 25 × 20 cm/10 × 8 in with microwave-proof cling film.

2 Cook the spinach without any excess water: place it in a large bowl, cover and cook on full for 5–7 minutes. Drain very well and when all the liquid has been removed, chop the spinach very finely in a food processor or blender.

3 Add the butter, egg yolks, grated nutmeg and salt and pepper to taste to the spinach. Mix together very well. Whisk the egg whites until they are stiff. Fold a spoonful of the beaten whites into

Mimosa Beans

the spinach mixture to lighten it and then fold in the remaining whites. Mix through carefully. Turn the mixture into the dish and cook on medium for 15 minutes.

4 Meanwhile, mix the curd cheese with the soured cream and spring onions. Season to taste. Have a clean tea towel spread on a board and when the roulade is cooked, turn it upside down onto the tea towel. Carefully peel off the film.

5 Spread the cheese and soured cream mixture over the spinach, taking care not to tear the surface. Using the tea towel to help you, roll the spinach up into a roll and onto a serving plate. Serve immediately. Although this is usually served hot, it is also very good cold.

Mimosa Beans

SERVES 4

POWER SETTING: FULL

450 g/1 lb French beans, trimmed

2 tbsp water

4 hard-boiled eggs

25 g/1 oz butter

1 tsp chopped sage

1 tbsp chopped parsley

salt and freshly ground black pepper

250 ml/8 fl oz natural yogurt

1 Place the beans in a large casserole. Add the water and cook, covered, on full for 5 minutes. Stir, then cook for a further 5 minutes. Allow to stand for 2 minutes and test to see if the beans are done.

2 While the beans are cooking, cut two eggs into rings, and sieve, separately, the yolks and whites of the other two. Mix the butter with the herbs and some pepper.

3 Add the butter to the beans and mix well, cook on full for 2 minutes. Pour the yogurt over the hot beans and garnish with sieved and sliced egg. Heat on full for 30 seconds, then serve.

Green Beans and Red Peppers

SERVES 4

POWER SETTING: FULL

450 g/1 lb green beans, trimmed and sliced

50 ml/2 fl oz water

2 tbsp vegetable oil

1 onion, finely chopped

1 red pepper, seeded and diced

1 clove garlic, crushed

4 tomatoes, peeled (see Cook's Tip, page 26) and chopped

2 tsp chopped sage or basil

1 Place the beans in a deep dish with the water, cover and cook on full for 4 minutes. Allow to stand for 2 minutes.

2 Mix the vegetable oil, onion, red pepper, garlic and tomatoes in a dish. Stir and cook on full for 6 minutes.

3 Drain the beans, place on a suitable serving dish and season well. Add the pepper mixture and sprinkle with chopped sage or basil. Cover and cook on full for 5 minutes. Allow to stand for 2–3 minutes, then serve.

Courgette Gratin

SERVES 4—6

POWER SETTINGS: FULL AND MEDIUM

450 g/1 lb courgettes, sliced

225 g/8 oz short-cut macaroni

1.15 L/2 pt boiling water

1 tbsp oil

1 large onion, chopped

1 (425-g/15-oz) can tomatoes

1 tsp dried basil, thyme or marjoram

a sliver of lemon peel

salt and freshly ground black pepper

2 eggs

150 ml/¼ pt natural yogurt

75 g/3 oz Cheddar cheese, grated

1 Place the courgettes in a dish, cover and cook on full for 5–6 minutes, or until tender. Stir half-way through the cooking time.

2 Place the macaroni in a large bowl. Pour in the boiling water and cook on full for 10 minutes. Set aside for 5 minutes, then drain.

3 In a basin, mix the oil and onion and cook on full for 3 minutes. Add the tomatoes, herb, lemon peel and seasoning. Cook on full for 5 minutes, stirring once to break up the tomatoes.

4 Mix the tomato sauce with the macaroni and spoon this into the base of suitable serving dish. Spoon the courgettes over the top in an even layer.

5 Beat the eggs, yogurt and half the cheese and spoon this over the courgettes. Cook on medium for 8–10 minutes or until the topping has almost set.

6 Sprinkle the remaining cheese over the top and brown the gratin under a hot grill. Serve at once.

Fennel with Parmesan

SERVES 4

POWER SETTING: FULL

2 bulbs fennel

50 g/2 oz butter

1 tbsp lemon juice

salt and freshly ground black pepper

2 tbsp grated Parmesan cheese

2 tbsp chopped fresh herbs (optional)

1 Remove the tough outer leaves from the bulbs of fennel, but reserve the feathery fronds. Slice the fennel.

2 Put the butter in a dish and cook on full for 1 minute. Add the fennel and turn it in the butter. Cover and cook on full for about 10 minutes, stirring twice, until the fennel is tender.

3 Sprinkle in the lemon juice, season with salt and pepper and spoon over the Parmesan cheese.

4 Garnish with the fennel fronds, and chopped fresh herbs (if used), then serve at once.

VEGETABLES

75

Spicy Stuffed Courgettes

SERVES 4–6

POWER SETTINGS: FULL AND MEDIUM

6 courgettes, halved lengthways

475 ml/16 fl oz water

salt and freshly ground black pepper

1 tbsp lemon juice

100 g/4 oz long-grain rice

1 onion, chopped

1 red pepper, seeded and chopped

100 ml/4 fl oz vegetable oil

1 clove garlic, crushed

2 tomatoes, peeled (see Cook's Tip, page 26), and chopped

1 tsp curry powder

100 g/4 oz mushrooms, chopped

150 ml/¼ pt soured cream

1 tsp paprika

1 tbsp chopped parsley or coriander leaves

1 Place the courgettes in a dish with 100 ml/4fl oz of the water. Cover and cook on full for 4 minutes. Drain and sprinkle with seasoning and lemon juice.

2 Place the rice in a casserole with the remaining water and season to taste. Cook on full for 12 minutes, then allow to stand for 3 minutes or until the rice has absorbed the water. If all the water has not been absorbed, then cook for a further 2 minutes.

3 Mix the onion and pepper with three-quarters of the oil and the crushed garlic. Cook on full for 4 minutes before stirring in the chopped tomatoes, curry powder and mushrooms.

4 Scoop out the inside of the courgettes. Chop the flesh and add to vegetable mixture. Cook on full for 4 minutes, stir well and season.

5 Mix the rice with the vegetable mixture and add half of the soured cream. Taste for seasoning.

6 Brush the courgettes with oil and spoon the stuffing into the shells. Arrange in a flat oiled dish and cook on full for 5 minutes, and then on medium for 5 minutes. Cook in two batches if the courgettes are large.

7 Top the courgettes with the remaining cream, a little paprika and chopped parsley or coriander.

Stuffed Mushrooms

SERVES 4

POWER SETTING: FULL

12 large open mushrooms

50 g/2 oz butter

1 onion, chopped

2 tomatoes, peeled (see Cook's Tip, page 26)

50 g/2 oz raisins

25 g/1 oz pine nuts

50 g/2 oz fresh breadcrumbs

1 tbsp chopped parsley

salt and pepper

1 egg

1 tsp paprika

1 Cut off the tips of the mushroom stalks, leaving a little piece of stalk in the mushroom as this helps to hold them together. Chop the remaining stalks.

2 Melt 25 g/1 oz butter on full for 1 minute. Add the onion and mushroom stalks, cook on full for 2 minutes.

3 Chop the tomatoes, add them to the onion mixture and cook for a further 1 minute on full.

4 Mix in all the other ingredients except the paprika and bind with the beaten egg. Pile the mixture onto the mushroom caps. Dot with the remaining butter.

5 Arrange half the mushroom caps on a buttered dish and cook, covered, for 3 minutes on full,

Stuffed Mushrooms

pause for 1 minute and continue cooking for another 3 minutes. Keep warm while the remainder of the mushrooms are cooked. Serve sprinkled with a little paprika.

Stuffed Peppers

SERVES 4

POWER SETTING: FULL

4 green, red or yellow peppers

100 g/4 oz long-grain rice

450 ml/¾ pt boiling beef stock

1 onion, finely chopped

1 clove garlic, finely chopped

salt and freshly ground black pepper

1 tsp dried mixed herbs

1 tbsp tomato purée

50 g/2 oz cooked ham, finely chopped

1 Cut off and reserve a slice from the top of each pepper. Remove the core and seeds from the middle of the peppers.

2 Stand the peppers in a dish and cook on full for 5–6 minutes, rearranging them once.

3 Place the rice, stock, onion, garlic, seasoning, herbs and tomato purée in a dish. Cover and cook on full for 12 minutes, or until all the stock has been absorbed.

4 Stir the ham into the rice then fill the peppers with the mixture and put on their lids. Cook for a further 4 minutes and allow to stand for 3–5 minutes before serving.

Stuffed Peppers

Dal

SERVES 4

POWER SETTING: FULL

225 g/8 oz red lentils

450 ml/¾ pt boiling water

2 slices fresh root ginger

pinch of turmeric

pinch of salt

1–2 tbsp sunflower oil

1 tsp mustard seeds

1 clove garlic, crushed

1 green chilli, seeded and chopped

pinch of garam masala

green chilli rings to garnish

pitta bread to serve

1 Put the lentils in a large dish and pour in the boiling water. Add the ginger, turmeric and salt, cover and cook on full for 12–15 minutes, stirring twice. Add a little extra boiling water if necessary during cooking.

2 Leave the dal to stand, covered for 5 minutes. Put the oil in a bowl and cook on full for 1 minute. Add the mustard seeds, garlic and chilli. Cover and continue to cook for 2 minutes.

3 Stir the oil dressing and garam masala into the dal. Garnish with the chilli rings and serve with warmed pitta bread.

MICROWAVE TIP

Red lentils cook very well in the microwave, but you do need to put them in a large dish to allow the liquid to boil up without spilling over. | A very deep, lidded casserole dish is ideal, otherwise use a suitable mixing bowl or large basin covered with a dinner plate.

Winter Vegetable Casserole

SERVES 4

POWER SETTING: FULL

25 g/1 oz butter

1 onion, chopped

1 potato, sliced

2 carrots, diced

1 parsnip, diced

1 leek, washed and sliced

1 red pepper, seeded and sliced

½ tsp dried thyme

½ tsp dried marjoram

1 tbsp tomato purée

250 ml/8 fl oz boiling vegetable stock

salt and freshly ground black pepper

1 tsp soy sauce

50 g/2 oz cheese, grated

1 tbsp chopped parsley

1 Place the butter and onion in a dish and cook on full for 3 minutes.

2 Place the potato, carrots, parsnip and leek in a bowl. Cover and cook on full for 5 minutes. Drain off any cooking liquid.

3 Add the blanched vegetables and pepper to the onion and cook for 3 minutes on full. Add the thyme, marjoram, tomato purée and stock. Season well, add the soy sauce, stir and cook on full for 15 minutes.

4 Check the vegetables at this stage to see if they are cooked to your liking: they will still be crunchy. Cook for a further 2 minutes if necessary. Serve hot sprinkled with cheese and parsley.

2 Pour the oil into a casserole and cook on full for 1 minute. Add the onion and garlic and cook for a further 1 minute. Stir in the peppers, aubergine and courgettes and cook on full for 5 minutes, stirring once.

3 Stir in the mushrooms, tomatoes, tomato purée, herbs, bay leaf and seasoning. Cover and cook on full for 15 minutes, stirring twice. Stir in the mozzarella. Cover and cook on full for 5 minutes, or until the cheese has melted. Serve with French bread to soak up the delicious juices.

Curried Vegetables

SERVES 4
POWER SETTING: FULL
225 g/8 oz aubergine, trimmed and cut into chunks
2 tbsp oil
1 onion, chopped
1 clove garlic, crushed
2 tsp curry powder
1 large potato, cut into chunks
100 g/4 oz green beans, trimmed
150 ml/¼ pt boiling water
100 g/4 oz tomatoes, quartered
1 tbsp garam masala
2 tsp cornflour
1 tbsp cold water
salt and freshly ground black pepper
150 ml/¼ pt natural yogurt
50 g/2 oz cashew nuts, roasted

1 Salt the aubergine and leave for 30 minutes. Rinse and pat dry.

2 Place the oil, onion and garlic in a casserole and cook on full for 3 minutes. Add the curry powder and stir in the potato. Cook, covered, on full for 8–10 minutes, stirring once, until the potato is tender.

3 Add the aubergine and cook for a further 5 minutes. Stir in the beans, boiling water, tomatoes and garam masala. Cover and cook on full for 10–12 minutes, stirring once, until tender.

4 Mix the cornflour to a smooth paste with the cold water and stir it into the curry. Cook on full for 2 minutes, stir and season to taste, then serve swirled with yogurt and topped with cashew nuts.

Ratatouille alla Mozzarella

SERVES 4
POWER SETTING: FULL
1 large aubergine, trimmed and sliced
3 courgettes, sliced
4 tbsp olive oil
1 large onion, sliced
2 cloves garlic, chopped
1 small red pepper, seeded and chopped
1 small green pepper, seeded and chopped
100 g/4 oz mushrooms, sliced
1 (425-g/15-oz) can tomatoes, mashed with their juice
1 tbsp tomato purée
2 tsp chopped mixed fresh herbs
1 bay leaf
salt and freshly ground black pepper
100 g/4 oz mozzarella cheese, cubed

1 Place the aubergine and courgettes in a colander, sprinkle with salt and allow to stand for 30 minutes. Rinse in cold water and pat dry on absorbent kitchen paper. Cut the aubergine into bite-sized pieces.

Aubergine and Rice Casserole

SERVES 4–6

POWER SETTING: FULL

2 aubergines, sliced lengthways

salt

juice of 1 lemon

225 g/8 oz long-grain rice

600 ml/1 pt boiling water

4 tbsp vegetable oil

2 onions, finely chopped

2 cloves garlic, crushed

1 carrot, grated

1 (425-g/15-oz) can tomatoes

1 tsp tomato purée

4 tbsp dry white wine

4 tbsp stock or water

1 tsp dried basil or 2 tsp chopped fresh basil

100 g/4 oz mushrooms, wiped and sliced

4 tbsp grated cheese (preferably Parmesan)

1 Arrange the aubergines on a tray lined with absorbent kitchen paper. Sprinkle with a little salt and lemon juice. Allow to stand for 20–30 minutes.

2 Place the rice and water in a bowl. Cover and cook on full for 15–20 minutes. Place in the bottom of an oiled casserole, or suitable dish.

3 Place half the oil, with the onions and garlic in a bowl and cook on full for 3 minutes. Add the grated carrot and cook for a further 3 minutes.

4 Add the tomatoes, tomato purée, white wine and stock or water with the basil. Stir until the tomatoes are broken down. Cook on full for 10–12 minutes.

5 Pat the sliced aubergine dry with absorbent kitchen paper. Place in a roasting bag with the remaining oil. Close the bag with an elastic band or plastic tie and cook on full for 10 minutes, rearranging once.

6 Place slices of aubergine over the rice. Season well. Add half the tomato sauce. Top with a layer of sliced mushrooms. Pour over the remaining tomato sauce. Add a final layer of aubergines. Cover and cook on full for 7–10 minutes, until bubbling hot.

7 Sprinkle the cheese on top and cook under a hot grill until golden.

Spicy Okra

SERVES 4-6

POWER SETTING: FULL

4 tbsp oil

1 large onion, chopped

1 chilli, seeded and chopped

2 tsp cumin seeds

2 tsp coriander seeds, lightly crushed

2 cloves garlic, crushed

450 g/1 lb okra, trimmed

2 tomatoes, peeled and chopped

¼ tsp salt

¼ tsp sugar

2 tbsp lemon juice

150 ml/¼ pt boiling water

1 Blend 1 tbsp oil, the onion, chilli, cumin and coriander seeds with the garlic in a food processor or blender. Add a few drops of water if the paste is too thick. Place in a small basin and cook on full for 3 minutes. Set aside.

2 Heat the remaining oil in a large casserole dish on full for about 1 minute. Add the okra, tomatoes, salt, sugar and lemon juice, and mix well. Pour in the water. Cook on full for 5 minutes.

3 Stir in the paste and cook for a further 5–7 minutes, or until the okra is cooked. The okra should be tender but not too soft as it becomes slimy on overcooking.

Vegetable Loaf

SERVES 6

POWER SETTINGS: FULL AND MEDIUM

225 g/8 oz broccoli spears

2 tbsp water

2 carrots, grated

3 celery sticks, cut into 2.5-cm/1-in pieces

25 g/1 oz butter

25 g/1 oz flour

3 eggs

salt and pepper

¼ tsp paprika

¼ tsp mustard powder

100 g/4 oz cottage cheese

100 g/4 oz Cheddar cheese, grated

2 tomatoes, peeled (see Cook's Tip, page 26) and sliced

2 spring onions, chopped

1 Arrange the broccoli spears in a ring on a shallow dish with heads to the centre of the dish. Sprinkle with the water, cover and cook on full for 8 minutes.

2 Arrange the carrot and celery between the broccoli. Cover and cook for 5 minutes on full, then drain.

3 Melt the butter in a bowl for 1 minute on full. Stir in the flour, gradually beat in the eggs and season well with salt, pepper, paprika and mustard. Beat in the cottage cheese and the grated cheese. Add the vegetables and cook on full for 3 minutes, stir well.

4 Butter a 450-g/1-lb loaf dish. Cover the bottom of the dish with the tomatoes and chopped spring onions, then pour in the mixture pressing it down well. Cover and cook on full for 3 minutes.

5 Reduce the power to medium and cook for a further 6 minutes. Leave to stand for 3 minutes. The loaf should be firmly set: if not, cook for a few minutes longer on medium, checking every minute.

6 Turn out the cooked loaf and serve cut into slices.

Vegetable Loaf

Rice and Pasta

All types of rice cook very well in the microwave. The cooking time is not enormously reduced, but the grains do not stick and burn and there is less chance of the liquid frothing up and boiling over.
● Remember to put the grains and liquid in a big dish or mixing bowl to allow for boiling.
● Cook closely covered, with a little seasoning.
● Leave the rice to stand for 5 minutes, then fluff up the grains with a fork before serving.

Pasta can also be cooked well in the microwave and small amounts are very successful.
● You will need a large dish to hold the pasta and plenty of water.
● Always add boiling water and make sure there is room for the water to boil and for the pasta to expand.

● If you are cooking lots of pasta – particularly spaghetti – it is probably best to use a very large saucepan on the conventional hob. Follow the charts for timings when cooking rice and pasta.

Time and Settings for Pasta and Grains

Although there are no real time savings in cooking rice and pasta in the microwave, there is no risk of them sticking to the pan. Standing is usually necessary to complete cooking.

Cooking times vary according to the type of pasta. Fresh pasta needs microwaving for only 1 minute. It requires no standing time, but should be drained and served immediately. Times for dried pasta and rice are given below.

Pasta and Grains Cooking Guide

RICE OR PASTA	BOILING WATER TO BE ADDED PER 225 G/8 OZ	MINUTES ON FULL PER 225 G/8 OZ	STANDING MINUTES
long-grain rice, untreated	750 ml/1¼ pt	14	5
American long-grain rice, easy-cook	900 ml/1½ pt	12	5
brown rice	900 ml/1½ pt	30	5
egg noodles and tagliatelle	1 L/1¾ pt with 2 teaspoons oil	6–8	2–3
spaghetti	1 L/1¾ pt with 2 teaspoons oil	12	5–10
pasta shells and shapes	1 L/1¾ pt with 2 teaspoons oil	12–14	5–10
macaroni	1 L/1¾ pt with 2 teaspoons oil	12–15	2–3
lasagne	1 L/1¾ pt with 2 teaspoons oil	9	2

Pasta Shells with Crab Meat

SERVES 4

POWER SETTING: FULL

400 g/14 oz pasta shells

about 1.25 L/2¼ pt boiling water

salt and freshly ground black pepper

1 tsp oil

200 g/7 oz crab meat, flaked

150 ml/¼ pt single cream

1 tbsp Marsala

cayenne pepper or paprika

chopped parsley to garnish

1 Put the pasta shells in a deep bowl and pour in boiling water to cover. Add a pinch of salt and the oil, then cover and cook on full for 9 minutes. Allow to stand still covered, while you make the sauce.

2 Stir the crab meat into the cream, add the Marsala and cook on full for 3 minutes.

3 Drain the pasta and stir in the sauce. Sprinkle with cayenne pepper or paprika and garnish with chopped parsley, then serve at once.

Macaroni Cheese with Tuna Fish

Macaroni Cheese with Tuna Fish

SERVES 4

POWER SETTING: FULL

225 g/8 oz short-cut macaroni

600 ml/1 pt boiling water

1 tbsp oil

salt and freshly ground black pepper

25 g/1 oz butter

25 g/1 oz plain flour

300 ml/½ pt milk

75 g/3 oz Edam cheese, grated

1 (198-g/7-oz) can tuna, drained and flaked

tomato slices to garnish

1 Place the macaroni in a bowl with the water, oil and a pinch of salt. Cover and cook on full for 10 minutes. Allow to stand for 3 minutes, then drain.

2 Place the butter in a bowl and cook for 1 minute. Stir in the flour and milk. Cook on full for 6 minutes, stirring every minute.

3 Stir in the cheese, tuna fish, macaroni and seasoning. Cook on full for 3–4 minutes, then brown the top under a hot grill. Garnish with tomato.

Spaghetti Bolognese

SERVES 4

POWER SETTING: FULL

2 tbsp oil

1 onion, chopped

2 cloves garlic, chopped

1 stick celery, chopped

1 carrot, chopped

½ green pepper, seeded and chopped

100 g/4 oz mushrooms, chopped

4 rashers streaky bacon, rind removed and diced

450 g/1 lb minced beef

1 (425-g/15-oz) can tomatoes

1 tbsp tomato purée

1 tsp dried mixed herbs

salt and freshly ground black pepper

1 tbsp red wine

275 g/10 oz spaghetti

about 1.5 L/2¾ pt boiling water

15 g/½ oz butter

grated Parmesan cheese, to serve

1 Place the oil in a large bowl and cook on full for 1 minute. Add the onion, garlic, celery, carrot, pepper and mushrooms and continue to cook for a further 3 minutes.

Spaghetti Bolognese

2 Stir in the bacon and cook on full for 3 minutes, then add the beef, tomatoes, tomato purée, herbs, seasoning and red wine. Cook on full for 12 minutes.

3 Place the spaghetti in a deep bowl, breaking it as necessary, and pour in the water, adding enough to cover the pasta. Cook, covered, for 8–10 minutes until just tender. Allow to stand, covered, for a further 8–10 minutes.

4 Re-heat the sauce on full for 2 minutes. Drain the spaghetti, toss it in butter and season with freshly ground black pepper. Serve in warmed individual pasta bowls topped with bolognese sauce. Offer Parmesan cheese to sprinkle on top.

Chicken Lasagne

Chicken Lasagne

SERVES 4
POWER SETTING: FULL
350 g/12 oz boneless chicken, skinned
175 g/6 oz lasagne
900 ml/1½ pt boiling water
salt and freshly ground black pepper
2 tsp oil
40 g/1½ oz butter
1 onion, chopped
1 clove garlic, chopped
100 g/4 oz mushrooms, sliced
1 tsp dried basil
40 g/1½ oz plain flour
450 ml/¾ pt milk
1 chicken stock cube
40 g/1½ oz Edam cheese, grated
fresh basil sprigs to garnish

1 Place the chicken in a shallow dish. Cover and cook on full for 7 minutes, turning once. Allow to stand, covered, for 5 minutes, then chop the meat.

2 Place the lasagne in a large oblong dish and cover completely with the water. Add a pinch of salt and the oil. Cover and cook on full for 10 minutes. Allow to stand, covered, for 15 minutes. Drain and lay out on a clean tea towel.

3 Place the butter in a bowl and cook on full for 1 minute. Stir in the onion, garlic, mushrooms and basil and continue to cook for 2 minutes.

4 Stir in the flour and gradually add the milk, stirring. Crumble in the stock cube, then cook on full for 4 minutes. Stir in the chicken, season with pepper and continue to cook for a further 3 minutes.

5 Layer the lasagne and chicken sauce in the casserole dish, starting with a layer of lasagne and ending with a layer of sauce. Top with the grated cheese. Cook on full for 1–2 minutes.

6 Brown the lasagne under the grill, garnish with sprigs of fresh basil, and serve piping hot.

Pasta Shells with Ham and Mushrooms

Pasta Shells with Ham and Mushrooms

SERVES 4
POWER SETTINGS: MEDIUM-HIGH AND FULL
350 g/12 oz pasta shells
900 ml/1½ pt boiling water
salt and freshly ground black pepper
1 tbsp oil
50 g/2 oz butter
1 small onion, chopped
1 stick celery, chopped
75 g/3 oz mushrooms, sliced
25 g/1 oz plain flour
300 ml/½ pt milk
175–225 g/6–8 oz cooked ham, diced
50 g/2 oz unsalted peanuts
chopped parsley to garnish

1 Place the pasta in a large bowl, pour in the boiling water, then add a pinch of salt and the oil. Cook on medium-high for 8–10 minutes or until barely tender. Drain, rinse with hot water and set aside.

2 Place the butter in a large casserole and cook on full for 1 minute. Stir in the onion, celery and mushrooms, and continue to cook for 3 minutes. Stir in the flour, then gradually stir in the milk.

Cook on full for 3 minutes, stirring every minute until thickened. Season to taste.

3 Stir in the pasta shells, ham and nuts, then cook on medium-high for 8–10 minutes. Allow to stand for 5 minutes before serving, sprinkled with the parsley.

Hay and Straw

Hay and Straw

SERVES 4
POWER SETTING: FULL
200 g/7 oz yellow tagliatelle
200 g/7 oz green tagliatelle
about 1.25 L/2¼ pt boiling water
salt and freshly ground black pepper
1 tsp oil
100 g/4 oz Parma ham, chopped
150 ml/¼ pt single cream
grated Parmesan cheese, to serve

1 Put the yellow and green tagliatelle together in a deep bowl and pour in enough boiling water to cover. Add a pinch of salt and the oil. Cover and cook on full for 6 minutes. Allow to stand, still covered, while you make the sauce.

2 Stir the ham and cream together in a bowl and season with black pepper. Cook on full for 2 minutes.

3 Drain the pasta, stir in the sauce and serve with a bowl of grated Parmesan cheese.

COOK'S TIP
Delicate Parma ham gives this pasta dish an authentic flavour;	*however, it is expensive and cooked ham can be substituted.*

Pasta with Chick Peas

Pasta with Chick Peas

SERVES 4

POWER SETTING: FULL

400 g/14 oz multi-coloured pasta

about 1.25 L/2¼ pt boiling water

salt and freshly ground black pepper

2 tbsp oil

25 g/1 oz butter

1 clove garlic, crushed

1 (400-g/14-oz) can chick peas, drained

50–75 g/2–3 oz Parmesan cheese, grated

1 Put the pasta in a bowl and pour in enough boiling water to cover. Add a pinch of salt and 1 tsp of the oil. Cover and cook on full for 10 minutes. Allow to stand still covered.

2 Put the butter in a bowl and cook on full for 1 minute. Stir in the garlic and chick peas, cover and continue to cook for 2 minutes.

3 Drain the pasta. Pour over the remaining oil and the garlic chick peas. Add the Parmesan cheese. Stir and serve at once. Offer black pepper at the table.

Pasta with Early Summer Vegetables

Pasta with Early Summer Vegetables

SERVES 4
POWER SETTING: FULL
400 g/14 oz tagliatelle
about 1.75 L/3 pt boiling water
salt and freshly ground black pepper
1 tsp oil
100 g/4 oz shelled broad beans
100 g/4 oz shelled peas
100 g/4 oz French beans, topped, tailed and cut into pieces
150 ml/¼ pt single cream
chopped fresh herbs, to garnish
grated Parmesan cheese, to serve

1 Put the tagliatelle in a deep bowl and pour in enough boiling water to cover. Add a pinch of salt and the oil. Cover and cook on full for 6 minutes. Set aside, still covered.

2 Put the broad beans, peas and green beans in a bowl with 2 tbsp boiling water. Cover and cook on full for 5 minutes. Drain, then return the vegetables to the bowl and add the cream. Cover and cook for a further 3 minutes.

3 Drain the pasta, pour over the vegetable mixture and serve sprinkled with the chopped fresh herbs.

4 Offer Parmesan cheese and black pepper at the table.

Rigatoni with Borlotti Beans

SERVES 4
POWER SETTING: FULL
400 g/14 oz rigatoni or macaroni
about 1.25 L/2¼ pt boiling water
salt and freshly ground black pepper
2 tbsp olive oil
25 g/1 oz butter
1 clove garlic, crushed
1 (400-g/14-oz) can borlotti beans, drained
175 g/6 oz mozzarella cheese, diced
2 tbsp chopped parsley

1 Put the pasta in a deep bowl and pour in enough boiling water to cover it. Add a pinch of salt and 1 tsp of the oil. Cover and cook on full for 10 minutes. Set aside, still covered.

2 Put the remaining oil in a bowl with the butter, garlic and beans. Stir well, then cook on full for 3–4 minutes, until heated through.

3 Drain the pasta and stir in the bean mixture and cheese. Cover and cook on full for 1½ minutes, or until the mozzarella begins to melt.

4 Sprinkle with chopped parsley and serve. Offer black pepper at the table.

Rigatoni with Borlotti Beans

Mixed Vegetable Lasagne

SERVES 4

POWER SETTING: FULL

1 aubergine, trimmed and sliced

2 courgettes, sliced

salt and freshly ground black pepper

juice of 1 lemon

25 g/1 oz butter

1 clove garlic, crushed

3 tbsp vegetable oil

600 ml/1 pt Tomato Sauce (see page 111)

600 ml/1 pt Béchamel Sauce (see page 111)

16 sheets lasagne, pre-cooked

100 g/4 oz mushrooms, sliced

25 g/1 oz fresh breadcrumbs

25 g/1 oz grated Parmesan cheese

1 Sprinkle the aubergine and courgettes with salt and lemon juice. Allow to stand for 20 minutes. Rub a large square dish with the butter mixed with the garlic.

2 Drain the aubergines and courgettes and pat dry with absorbent kitchen paper. Place the oil in a flat dish and cook the aubergines and courgettes in batches allowing 3 minutes on full for each batch.

3 Place a little of the tomato and Béchamel sauces in a lasagne dish. Cover with the sheets of lasagne. Spread with a little tomato sauce and a layer of aubergine, courgettes and mushrooms. Top with Béchamel sauce.

4 Season well and continue layering the vegetables and pasta. Top with the remaining tomato and Béchamel sauce.

5 Cook on full for 10 minutes. Allow to stand for 5 minutes, then cook for a further 5 minutes on full.

6 Mix the breadcrumbs and Parmesan cheese, then sprinkle the mixture over the lasagne. Cook for a further 5 minutes on full. Brown under a hot grill if liked. Serve with green salad.

Cannelloni with Spinach and Ricotta

SERVES 4

POWER SETTING: FULL

350 g/12 oz cooked spinach, drained and chopped

225 g/8 oz ricotta cheese

¼ tsp grated nutmeg

salt and freshly ground black pepper

12 cannelloni tubes, cooked

1 (425-g/15-oz) can tomatoes, sieved

1 tsp dried basil or 2 tsp chopped fresh basil

25 g/1 oz butter

1 onion, chopped

¼ tsp dried oregano

600 ml/1 pt Béchamel Sauce (see page 111)

50 g/2 oz cheese, grated

1 tbsp chopped parsley

1 Mix the spinach with the ricotta cheese, nutmeg and seasoning. Spoon or pipe the mixture into the cannelloni tubes.

2 Season the tomatoes with salt, pepper and basil. Place in an even layer in the bottom of a dish.

3 Heat the butter on full in a small dish for 1 minute. Add the onion and cook on full for 3 minutes. Stir in oregano. Pour this over the tomato, then arrange the cannelloni tubes on top.

4 Coat with the Béchamel sauce and cook on full for 5 minutes. Top with the cheese, brown under a hot grill and serve garnished with parsley.

Plain Fried Rice

SERVES 4

POWER SETTING: FULL

3 tbsp vegetable oil

1 large onion, finely chopped

225 g/8 oz long-grain rice

600 ml/1 pt boiling chicken stock

salt and freshly ground black pepper

1 tbsp soy sauce

red pepper rings to garnish (optional)

1 Place the oil and onion in a bowl or casserole dish and cook on full for 3 minutes. Add the rice and stir well. Cover and cook the rice with the oil for 4–5 minutes, stirring once, until the grains begin to turn transparent.

2 Pour in the stock, add a little seasoning and cover the dish. Cook on full for 15–20 minutes, until all the stock has been absorbed.

3 Sprinkle with soy sauce and serve garnished with red pepper rings if you like.

VARIATIONS

This basic recipe can be varied by adding an assortment of tasty ingredients. It is an ideal dish for using leftovers, or it can be served with some shredded, plain egg omelette (cooked conventionally). About 5 minutes before the end of the cooking time, add peeled cooked prawns; drained, canned sliced bamboo shoots; drained, sliced canned water chestnuts; diced cooked chicken or ham, or a few chopped salted peanuts.

Pilau Rice

SERVES 4

POWER SETTING: FULL

225 g/8 oz basmati rice

2 tbsp vegetable oil

1 onion, finely chopped

1 clove garlic, crushed

½ tsp ground cumin

¼ tsp turmeric

½ red chilli, seeded and finely chopped (optional)

¼ tsp ground coriander

pinch of salt

600 ml/1 pt boiling stock or water

1 Wash the rice under running water, taking care not to damage the grains. Place the oil, onion and garlic in a bowl or casserole and cook on full for 3 minutes.

2 Add the rice, cumin, turmeric, chilli (if used) and coriander. Stir in the salt and boiling liquid. Cover and cook on full for 15–20 minutes, or until all the liquid has been absorbed. Fluff up the grains with a fork and serve.

VARIATION

Vegetable pilau can be made by adding peas, beans, carrots, peppers, potatoes or a combination of all favourite vegetables. It is advisable to cut the potatoes and carrots into small dice, and cook them for 2–4 minutes to ensure that they become cooked through. Add the chopped vegetables to the onion and garlic, and cook together for 5–7 minutes, depending on the quantity of vegetables and their type. For extra flavour add ½ tsp garam masala and fork in 2 tbsp chopped fresh coriander before serving the pilau.

COOK'S TIP

Basmati rice is available from good supermarkets, health food shops and ethnic stores. It is lightly scented and has a delicate flavour. Before cooking, the grains should be washed to remove excess starch. Place the rice in a basin, cover it with water and gently swirl the grains with your fingers. Drain and repeat three or four times, until the water runs clear.

Plain Fried Rice

Herbed Rice

SERVES 4

POWER SETTING: FULL

50 g/2 oz butter

1 clove garlic, crushed

1 onion, finely chopped

8 spring onions, sliced

225 g/8 oz long-grain rice

600 ml/1 pt boiling water

salt and freshly ground black pepper

4 tbsp chopped parsley

8 basil leaves, chopped

parsley sprigs to garnish

1 Place the butter, garlic and onion in a basin and cook on full for 4 minutes. Add the spring onions. Set aside.

2 Place the rice, water and a pinch of salt in a bowl. Cover and cook on full for 15–20 minutes, or until all the water has been absorbed.

3 Fork the onion mixture into the rice 5 minutes before the end of the cooking time. Cover and continue cooking.

4 Add the parsley and basil leaves. Season with freshly ground black pepper and extra salt, if necessary, and serve garnished with parsley sprigs.

Chicken Biriani

SERVES 4

POWER SETTING: FULL

225 g/8 oz basmati rice

2 large onions

2 cloves garlic, crushed

2.5-cm/1-in piece fresh root ginger, grated

6 tbsp vegetable oil

50 g/2 oz slivered almonds

2 boneless chicken breasts

¼ tsp chilli powder

1 tsp ground cumin

5 tbsp natural yogurt

1 tbsp lemon juice

1 tsp ground coriander

¼ tsp ground cinnamon

¼ tsp turmeric

900 ml/1½ pt boiling water

salt and freshly ground black pepper

GARNISH

1 hard-boiled egg, sliced

1 tomato, sliced

parsley sprigs

1 Wash the rice under running water, taking care not to damage the grains.

2 Slice half an onion finely into rings and reserve. Place the remaining onion, garlic, ginger and 1 tbsp oil in a blender or food processor with a few of the slivered almonds. Grind to a paste, adding a little water if necessary.

3 Skin the chicken and cut it into chunks, then toss them in the chilli powder.

4 Reserve 1 tbsp of the remaining oil, then place the rest in a large casserole dish with the paste. Cover, cook on full for 5 minutes, stirring once.

5 Add the chicken, cumin, yogurt and lemon juice and re-cover. Cook on full for 5 minutes, stir well and cook for a further 3 minutes.

6 Add rice, coriander, cinnamon and turmeric, then pour in the water and stir lightly. Season with a little salt and pepper, cover and cook on full for 15 minutes. Using a fork, lightly rearrange the ingredients, then re-cover and cook for 10 minutes or until the liquid has been absorbed.

Chicken Biriani

7 Heat the remaining oil in a frying pan on the conventional hob. Fry the reserved onion rings until golden, then drain them on absorbent kitchen paper. Lightly roast the remaining slivered almonds in the oiled frying pan.

8 Fork the almonds into the biriani and serve garnished with hard-boiled egg, tomato, parsley and the fried onion rings.

COOK'S TIP

Serve the biriani with Indian breads, a dish of spiced vegetables and a cucumber raita. To make a refreshing raita, | peel and dice ½ small cucumber and mix it with 150 ml/¼ pt natural yogurt. Add a little chopped fresh mint.

Chicken and Wild Rice Salad

SERVES 4
POWER SETTING: FULL
175 g/6 oz mixed long-grain and wild rice
600 ml/1 pt boiling water
225 g/8 oz cooked chicken, chopped
1 small onion
150 ml/¼ pt mayonnaise
100 g/4 oz mushrooms
1 tbsp lemon juice
4 tbsp sweet corn
7 black olives
salt and freshly ground black pepper
1 lettuce
2 heads chicory

1 Place the rice in a large bowl or casserole dish. Add the water, cover and cook on full for 25–30 minutes or until all the water has been absorbed and the rice is tender. Check halfway through cooking, giving the grains a light stir. Leave to cool completely.

2 Add the chicken to the cooled rice. Chop the onion finely and add to the mixture with the mayonnaise.

3 Slice the mushrooms thinly. Mix with the rice, remembering to save a few for the top of the salad. Pour the lemon juice over the reserved mushrooms.

4 Add the sweet corn and 4 chopped olives to the mixture. Season to taste. Arrange the lettuce and chicory in a salad bowl. Turn the chicken and rice mixture into the bowl. Garnish with the reserved mushroom slices and the remaining black olives.

Spanish Rice

SERVES 4

POWER SETTING: FULL

225 g/8 oz long-grain rice

600 ml/1 pt boiling stock or water

½ tsp turmeric

salt and freshly ground black pepper

2 tbsp vegetable oil

1 onion, finely chopped

2 red peppers, seeded and sliced

100 g/4 oz chicken livers, chopped

6 tomatoes, peeled (see Cook's Tip, page 26) and chopped

100 g/4 oz frozen petits pois

100 g/4 oz peeled cooked prawns

¼ tsp sugar

1 tbsp chopped parsley

1 Place the rice in a large bowl with the stock or water. Add the turmeric and a little salt. Cover and cook on full for 15 minutes, until the rice is almost cooked.

2 Place the oil, onion and peppers in a basin. Cover and cook on full for 5 minutes. Add the chicken livers, stir, cover and cook for a further 3 minutes.

3 Add the chicken liver mixture to the rice with the tomatoes, petits pois and prawns. Sprinkle in the sugar and fork the ingredients into the rice which should still be quite moist. If it has dried up on standing, add a little extra water.

4 Cover and cook on full for a further 7–10 minutes, until all the ingredients are cooked and the liquid has been absorbed.

5 Serve sprinkled with chopped parsley.

Stuffed Tomatoes

SERVES 4

POWER SETTING: FULL

2 tbsp oil

1 large onion, chopped

1 green pepper, seeded and chopped

1 green chilli, seeded and sliced

50 g/2 oz long-grain rice

½ tsp curry powder

150 ml/¼ pt boiling water

4 large tomatoes

50 g/2 oz cooked beef, lamb or chicken, finely chopped

1 spring onion, chopped

25 g/1 oz blanched almonds, chopped

1 tsp chopped parsley or coriander

parsley sprigs to garnish

1 Place the oil, onion, green pepper and chilli in a basin and cook on full for 4 minutes. Add the rice, curry powder and water, and continue to cook on full, covered, for 12–15 minutes, or until all the liquid has been absorbed. Set aside for 15 minutes.

2 Cut the tops off the tomatoes, scoop out their centres and sieve the pulp with the tomato tops. Add the sieved pulp to the rice. Leave the hollowed tomatoes upside-down on absorbent kitchen paper to drain completely.

3 Stir the meat, spring onion, almonds and parsley or coriander into the rice. Season to taste and use a teaspoon to spoon this stuffing into the tomatoes.

4 Arrange the tomatoes in a shallow dish and cook on full for 3–5 minutes, until hot through. Serve at once, garnished with parsley.

Jambalaya

SERVES 4

POWER SETTING: FULL

25 g/1 oz butter

2 tbsp oil

1 onion, finely chopped

4 sticks celery, chopped

1 green pepper, seeded and diced

2 aubergines, trimmed and diced

225 g/8 oz long-grain rice

600 ml/1 pt boiling chicken stock

salt and freshly ground black pepper

1 tbsp Worcestershire sauce

1 tsp soy sauce

100 g/4 oz cooked ham, diced

225 g/8 oz peeled cooked prawns

3 tbsp chopped parsley

GARNISH

4 whole cooked prawns

4 lemon wedges

1 Place the butter, oil and onion in a casserole dish and cook on full for 3 minutes. Stir in the celery, pepper and aubergine. Cover and continue to cook on full for 5–6 minutes.

2 Stir in the rice. Pour in the stock, add seasoning, the Worcestershire sauce and soy sauce. Cover and cook on full for 15 minutes.

3 Lightly stir in the ham and prawns. Re-cover the dish and cook on full for 5–10 minutes, or until all the liquid has been absorbed.

4 Taste for seasoning and fork up the ingredients, adding the parsley. Serve at once, garnished with whole prawns and lemon wedges.

Risotto

SERVES 4

POWER SETTING: FULL

50 g/2 oz butter

1 large onion, chopped

1 courgette, diced

1 carrot, diced

50 g/2 oz frozen peas

50 g/2 oz tomatoes, peeled and chopped

50 g/2 oz mushrooms, sliced

400 g/14 oz long-grain rice

750 ml/1¾ pt boiling chicken stock

1 tbsp tomato purée

½ tsp oil

salt and freshly ground black pepper

1 tbsp chopped fresh herbs

1 Place the butter in a large bowl and cook for 1 minute. Stir in the vegetables, cover and cook on full for 8 minutes, stirring once.

2 Add the rice, stir in the stock, tomato purée, oil and seasoning to taste. Cover and cook on full for 15 minutes, stirring once.

3 Allow to stand, covered, for 7 minutes. Fluff up the risotto with a fork and garnish with the herbs.

Savoury Spinach Rice

SERVES 4

POWER SETTING: FULL

25 g/1 oz butter

1 tbsp oil

1 onion, chopped

1 leek, trimmed, washed and sliced

450 g/1 lb frozen leaf spinach, partly thawed

225 g/8 oz long-grain rice

600 ml/1 pt boiling water or stock

juice of ½ lemon

salt and freshly ground black pepper

¼ tsp grated nutmeg

1 tbsp chopped parsley

1 tbsp natural yogurt (optional)

1 Place the butter, oil, onion and leek in a bowl and cover. Cook on full for 5 minutes.

2 Add the spinach, breaking up the blocks into chunks. Cover and cook on full for 5–6 minutes or until the spinach is almost fully thawed.

3 Add the rice and stir it in with the vegetables. Add the water or stock, lemon juice, seasoning and nutmeg. Cover and cook on full for 20–25 minutes or until the rice is cooked and the liquid has been absorbed.

4 Fluff up the rice and serve sprinkled with parsley. A little yogurt can be swirled onto the rice, if liked.

Dolmades

MAKES ABOUT 60

POWER SETTINGS: FULL AND MEDIUM

1 packet preserved vine leaves

300 ml/½ pt plus 2 tbsp boiling water

2 tbsp oil

2 large onions, finely chopped

225 g/8 oz risotto rice

25 g/1 oz pine nuts, chopped

4 tbsp chopped parsley

1 tsp chopped fresh mint

2 tbsp currants

salt and freshly ground black pepper

175 g/6 oz cooked lamb, minced or finely chopped (optional)

150 ml/¼ pt salad oil

juice of 2 lemons

lemon wedges to garnish

1 Rinse the vine leaves, place in a roasting bag with the 2 tbsp water and cook on full for 5 minutes.

2 Place the oil and onions in a bowl and cook on full for 3 minutes. Add the risotto rice and stir gently. Add the chopped pine nuts, parsley, mint, currants and seasoning. Gradually add the boiling water.

3 Cover and cook on full for about 10–12 minutes, until the water is absorbed. If you are adding the lamb, then stir it in at this stage.

4 Smooth the drained leaves on a board and place 1 tsp of stuffing in the centre of each one. Fold the stem end up and the sides in, and roll firmly.

5 Line a dish with any leaves which are not suitable for rolling and pack the rolls tightly into the dish seam-side down. Finish one layer and sprinkle with salad oil and lemon juice.

6 Continue packing layers until leaves are used up, sprinkling each with oil and lemon juice. Cover and cook on medium for 35–40 minutes, then leave to cool – excess liquid will be absorbed. Chill before serving.

7 To serve, place in a serving dish and garnish with lemon wedges.

Rice à la Provençal

SERVES 4

POWER SETTING: FULL

225 g/8 oz long-grain rice

600 ml/1 pt boiling water

salt and freshly ground black pepper

4 tbsp olive oil

25 g/1 oz butter

2 onions, finely chopped

2 cloves garlic, crushed

2 red peppers, seeded and sliced

4 courgettes, thinly sliced

½ tsp dried basil

4 tbsp dry white white

8 tomatoes, peeled and chopped

GARNISH

1 tbsp chopped capers

2 hard-boiled eggs, sliced

8 stuffed olives, sliced

2 tbsp chopped parsley or chervil

1 Place the rice and water in a large casserole with a pinch of salt. Cover and cook on full for 15–20 minutes, until all the water has been absorbed.

2 Place the oil, butter and onions in a bowl and cook on full for 4 minutes. Add the garlic and peppers and cook for a further 4 minutes. Stir in the courgettes, basil and wine, then cover and cook for 6–8 minutes, until all the vegetables are tender.

3 Lastly, stir in the tomatoes. Gently fold the vegetables into the cooked rice and season well. Serve at once, garnished with capers, hard-boiled eggs, olives and chopped parsley or chervil.

Prawn and Cucumber Salad

SERVES 4

POWER SETTING: FULL

225 g/8 oz long-grain rice

¼ tsp turmeric

600 ml/1 pt boiling water or chicken stock

salt and freshly ground black pepper

4 spring onions

½ cucumber

175 g/6 oz peeled cooked prawns

1 green pepper, seeded and sliced

juice of 1 lemon

150 ml/¼ pt vinaigrette dressing (see Cook's Tip, below)

GARNISH

whole cooked prawns

parsley sprigs

1 Place the rice, turmeric and water in a bowl. Add a pinch of salt, and cook on full for 15–20 minutes, until all the water has been absorbed. Leave to cool.

2 Chop the spring onions finely and add to the rice. Cut half the cucumber into thin slices to surround the rice when served. Chop the remainder into cubes and add to the rice mixture with the prawns.

3 Add the pepper to the rice mixture. Mix well with salt, pepper and lemon juice. Then add the dressing.

4 Arrange the salad on a plate and garnish with the reserved cucumber. Garnish with whole prawns and parsley sprigs.

Spiced Rice Salad

SERVES 4

POWER SETTING: FULL

225 g/8 oz long-grain rice

1 tsp garam masala

1 bay leaf

600 ml/1 pt boiling water

25 g/1 oz butter

1 clove garlic, crushed

1 onion, chopped

50 g/2 oz frozen peas

50 g/2 oz sultanas

1 green pepper, seeded and diced

salt and freshly ground black pepper

1 small lettuce

6 tbsp natural yogurt

GARNISH

2 tomatoes, cut into wedges

mustard and cress

orange slice

1 Place the rice, garam masala and bay leaf in a bowl. Pour in the water, cover and cook for 15 minutes, until all the water has been absorbed and the rice is tender. Leave to cool.

2 Place the butter, garlic and onion in a basin and cook on full for 3 minutes. Add the peas and cook for 2–3 minutes, until defrosted. Add to the rice.

3 Mix the sultanas, green pepper and seasoning to taste into the rice. Line a salad bowl with lettuce, then turn the rice salad into it. Top with yogurt and garnish with tomatoes, mustard and cress, and a slice of orange.

COOK'S TIP

You can buy bottled vinaigrette dressing, but home-made is nicer and it can be varied to suit your taste. In a screw-top jar mix 150 ml/¼ pt salad oil with 2–3 tbsp wine vinegar or cider vinegar. Add plenty of seasoning, 1 tsp Dijon mustard, ½ tsp caster sugar and a crushed clove of garlic if you like. Shake until the ingredients are thoroughly mixed. The dressing will keep in the refrigerator for 3 weeks.

Waldorf Rice Salad

SERVES 4

POWER SETTING: FULL

225 g/8 oz long-grain rice

¼ tsp turmeric

600 ml/1 pt boiling water or stock

1 small onion, finely chopped

6 sticks celery, sliced

4 spring onions, chopped

50 g/2 oz walnuts, chopped

1 red apple

1 green apple

juice of 1 lemon

150 ml/¼ pt mayonnaise

1 tbsp chopped parsley

1 lettuce heart

a few walnut halves to garnish

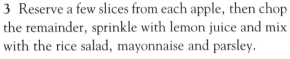

Waldorf Salad

1 Place the rice, turmeric and water or stock in a bowl. Cover and cook on full for 15–20 minutes, until all the water has been absorbed. Add the onion and leave until cold.

2 Add the celery, spring onions and walnuts to the rice and mix well.

3 Reserve a few slices from each apple, then chop the remainder, sprinkle with lemon juice and mix with the rice salad, mayonnaise and parsley.

4 Line a salad bowl with lettuce leaves, turn the rice salad into it and garnish with the reserved apple slices and walnut halves.

Spiced Rice Salad

Supper Dishes and Snacks

The microwave cooker is a plus when it comes to quick snacks, speedy scrambled eggs for breakfast or a quick dish for supper. This is where you will discover just how well the microwave performs when time is short and appetites are raging.

● Set aside portions of food to be reheated for supper or by members of the family who do not conform to eating at main meal times. Make sure they know the rules for reheating: cover the food, rearrange it during cooking, make sure it is thoroughly heated and leave it to stand for a few minutes before eating.

● As well as the recipes here, try heating canned or packet soups, baked beans or similar canned products or ready-made flans and quiches.

● For real emergencies it is a good idea to keep a few items in the freezer (flans, sauced dishes, pasties and so on) labelled with the name and date but adding a note as to how long they take to defrost and reheat in the microwave. This way any member of the family can plead complete kitchen ignorance but still cope with preparing a hot supper!

Garlic Prawns with Eggs

SERVES 4
POWER SETTING: MEDIUM
2 tbsp olive oil
1 large clove garlic, crushed
225 g/8 oz peeled cooked prawns
4 eggs
4 whole cooked prawns to garnish

1 Brush four ramekins or individual dishes generously with the oil. Sprinkle a little of the garlic in each dish.

2 Divide the prawns between the dishes and stir to coat them in the oil. Push the prawns to one side of the dishes, then break an egg into each.

3 Pierce the yolks carefully with a cocktail stick to prevent them bursting during cooking. Cover the dishes and cook on medium for about 3½ minutes, turning the dishes once.

4 Allow the eggs to stand for 1 minute, then garnish with prawns and serve with crusty bread.

Smoked Salmon Scrambled Eggs

SERVES 2
POWER SETTING: FULL
6 eggs
1 tbsp milk
freshly ground black pepper
100 g/4 oz smoked salmon, roughly chopped
25 g/1 oz butter
hot buttered toast, to serve
pinch of cayenne pepper to garnish

1 Beat the eggs with the milk and season with black pepper. Stir in the salmon.

2 Put the butter in a bowl and cook on full for 1 minute, until melted.

3 Stir in the eggs and smoked salmon. Cook on full for about 3 minutes, or until the eggs are just set, stirring every minute.

4 The cooked eggs should be thick and creamy: pile them onto hot toast and add a sprinkling of cayenne pepper.

Spicy Scrambled Eggs with Anchovies

SERVES 4
POWER SETTING: FULL
8 eggs
2 tbsp milk
½ tsp garam masala
freshly ground black pepper
1 (50-g/2-oz) can anchovy fillets, drained and chopped
25 g/1 oz butter
hot toast, to serve
parsley sprigs to garnish

1 Beat the eggs with the milk, garam masala and pepper. Stir in the anchovies.

2 Place the Butter in a bowl and cook on full for 1 minute. Stir in the egg mixture and cook on full for about 3–4 minutes, or until just set, stirring every minute.

3 Allow to stand for 1 minute before serving with triangles of hot toast, garnished with parsley sprigs if you like.

MICROWAVE TIP

Use this recipe as a guide when cooking plain scrambled eggs. Add 1 tbsp of milk to 2 eggs and season them, whisking well, before cooking. The secret for success when microwaving plain scrambled eggs is to whisk them regularly, every 45–60 seconds, during cooking; they will be rich and creamy.

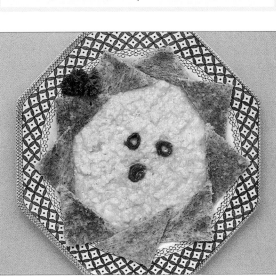

Spicy Scrambled Eggs with Anchovies

Eggs Florentine

SERVES 4

POWER SETTING: FULL

half quantity Creamed Spinach (see page 72)

4 eggs

salt and freshly ground black pepper

4 tbsp single cream

hot buttered toast, to serve

1 Butter four ramekin dishes and divide the spinach between them.

2 Make a well in the centre of each portion of spinach. Break the eggs into a cup one at a time and slide each into a bed of spinach. Prick the yolks with a skewer or cocktail stick, season with salt and pepper and carefully pour the cream over the top.

3 Stand the dishes in a deep glass dish. Pour some boiling water around them. Cook on full for 4 minutes. Check to see if the eggs are cooked; if not, cook for a further 1 minute or to taste.

4 Sprinkle with chopped parsley and serve with hot buttered toast.

MICROWAVE TIP

To cook one egg with spinach as above allow 1½ minutes on full.

Pipérade

Curried Eggs

SERVES 2

POWER SETTING: FULL

25 g/1 oz butter

1 onion, finely chopped

1 tbsp curry powder

1 tbsp cornflour

2 tbsp water

300 ml/½ pt natural yogurt

2 tbsp chutney

1 tbsp desiccated coconut

salt and freshly ground black pepper

4 hard-boiled eggs

1 In a basin mix the butter and onion. Cook on full for 4 minutes. Stir in the curry powder and continue to cook for 1 minute.

2 Mix the cornflour and water to a smooth paste and add it to the yogurt. Add this to the onion, stir well and cook on full for 4 minutes, until thickened.

3 Add the chutney and most of the coconut, then taste and adjust the seasoning.

4 Arrange the eggs on a plate, pour over the sauce and sprinkle the reserved coconut over. Serve at once with cooked rice.

Pipérade

SERVES 4

POWER SETTINGS: MEDIUM AND FULL

50 ml/2 fl oz vegetable oil

1 clove garlic

1 small onion, chopped

2 spring onions, sliced

1 red pepper, peeled, seeded and finely diced

1 green pepper, peeled, seeded and finely diced

1 bouquet garni

1 bay leaf

2 large tomatoes, peeled, seeded and finely chopped

salt and freshly ground black pepper

8 eggs

50 ml/2 fl oz water

25 g/1 oz butter, cut into small pieces

hot buttered toast, to serve

1 Place the oil, whole clove of garlic, onion and spring onion in a dish and cook on medium for 7 minutes.

2 Add the peppers, bouquet garni and bay leaf. Cover and cook on full for 5 minutes. Add the tomatoes, season well and cook on full for a further 5 minutes.

3 Beat the eggs with the water. Add the butter. Remove the bouquet garni, bay leaf and garlic from the tomato mixture and stir in the eggs. Cook on full for 4 minutes, remove and mix well.

4 Cook for a further 4 minutes. Remove and stir again. If the mixture is too liquid, cook for a further 2 minutes until the eggs are creamy – test after stirring. Serve with hot buttered toast.

MICROWAVE TIP

Remember that – like scrambled eggs – the mixture thickens very quickly and eggs can toughen if cooked for a few seconds too long, so check the pipérade frequently as it cooks.

Welsh Rarebit Special

SERVES 4

POWER SETTINGS: FULL AND MEDIUM

4 slices cooked ham

225 g/8 oz Cheddar cheese, grated

15 g/½ oz butter

salt and freshly ground black pepper

½ tsp Worcestershire sauce

3 tbsp single cream

½ tsp paprika

4 slices wholewheat bread

GARNISH

tomato wedges

watercress and parsley sprigs

1 Trim the fat off the ham. Place the cheese and butter in a bowl and cook on full, stirring every minute, for 3 minutes until the cheese has melted.

2 Stir in the seasoning, Worcestershire sauce, paprika and cream, then cook on medium for 8 minutes, stirring every minute, until smooth and creamy.

3 Meanwhile, toast the bread conventionally, top with the ham, then with the cheese mixture. Serve at once, garnished with tomato wedges, watercress and parsley.

Cheese Fondue

SERVES 4

POWER SETTING: FULL

1 clove garlic, finely chopped

150 ml/¼ pt dry white wine

225 g/8 oz Gruyère cheese, grated

2 tsp cornflour

2 tbsp brandy

freshly ground black pepper

pinch of grated nutmeg

1 Place the garlic and wine in a bowl and cook on full for 2 minutes. Add the cheese and cook on full for 4 minutes, stirring 3 times, until the cheese has melted.

2 Mix the cornflour with the brandy, pepper and nutmeg, then stir the mixture into the cheese and continue to cook for 4 minutes, until thickened and just boiling.

3 Serve with French bread cut into bite-sized pieces and accompany with a crisp salad. Provide each guest with a fondue fork or kebab stick for spearing the bread to dip into the hot cheese sauce.

MICROWAVE TIP

Many of the glazed earthenware fondue pots can be used in the microwave but remember to **avoid metal containers.** If your fondue is unsuitable for use in the microwave, try using a large soufflé dish which can be kept warm over a candle burner. If the fondue cools, reheat it on full for 30–60 seconds.

Pizza Base

Making a pizza using the microwave oven to prove the dough is even faster than making a pie or a flan. However the pizza is better cooked in a conventional oven for a crisp crust. A special browning dish is available in the shape of a pizza which will give a crisp base if the dish is heated for 5 minutes, then brushed over with oil. This dish is also useful for re-heating frozen pizza.

SERVES 4

POWER SETTING: FULL

450 g/1 lb strong flour

1 tsp salt

15 g/½ oz fresh yeast or 3 tsp dried yeast and ½ tsp sugar

300 ml/½ pt tepid water

1 tbsp oil

1 Sift the flour into a bowl with the salt. If using fresh yeast, cream the yeast with a little of the water, then gradually add the remainder. If using dried yeast, mix the sugar with the water. Sprinkle the yeast in and whisk. Leave for 10–15 minutes until frothy.

2 Add the yeast liquid to the flour with the oil and mix to a firm dough. Knead for 5–10 minutes, or until the dough is smooth and elastic. Clean the bowl, return the dough to it and cover with cling film. Cook on full for 15 seconds, then allow to stand for 10 minutes.

3 Microwave the dough for a further 15 seconds and allow to stand for another 10 minutes. Repeat this 15 second burst once more leaving to stand as before.

4 The dough should now have doubled in size and it is ready to be made into a pizza. It will make four 20-cm/8-in circles.

COOK'S TIP

This dough can also be made with wholewheat flour, or half wholewheat and half white flour.

Pizza Base with a variety of toppings

Pizza Napolitana

SERVES 4

POWER SETTING: FULL

4 rounds bread dough, about 20 cm/8 in. in diameter

50 ml/2 fl oz olive oil

1 clove garlic, peeled

2 (425-g/15-oz) cans tomatoes

salt and freshly ground black pepper

2 tsp chopped fresh basil or 1 tsp dried basil

24 black olives

225 g/8 oz mozzarella cheese, sliced

1 Prepare the pizza dough according to the instructions for Pizza Base. Preheat a conventional oven to 230°C/450°F/Gas mark 8. Oil two baking sheets or four flan rings. If you use flan rings you will have a deep dish pizza. Place the circles of dough on the trays. Brush the dough with olive oil.

2 Rub the dough with a cut clove of garlic. If you like a stronger flavour, crush the remainder of the garlic into the tomatoes.

3 Mash the tomatoes with a wooden spoon and season well. Add the chopped basil. Cover the rounds of dough with the tomato mixture. Arrange the black olives and mozzarella cheese on the top.

4 Brush the pizzas with more oil. Bake the pizzas for 12–15 minutes until crisp and brown.

MICROWAVE TIP

It is possible to cook a quick pizza in the microwave but it must be eaten quickly or the dough will become tough. Take a browning dish or pizza tray and heat according to the | *manufacturer's instructions. Brush with oil, lay the dough in the dish, cover it with the filling and cook on full for 5 minutes. Allow to stand for 3 minutes. The pizza is tasty but pale.*

Quick Ham and Bean Hash

Quick Ham and Bean Hash

SERVES 4

POWER SETTINGS: FULL AND MEDIUM

25 g/1 oz butter

4 rashers streaky bacon, rind removed and diced

1 onion, sliced

1 (400-g/14-oz) can new potatoes, drained and diced

1 (400-g/14-oz) can kidney beans, drained

1 (325-g/11.5-oz) can sweetcorn, drained

225 g/8 oz cooked ham, sliced

1 (425-g/15-oz) can tomatoes, finely chopped

2 tbsp tomato purée

1 tbsp Worcestershire sauce

1 tbsp soy sauce

Tabasco sauce to taste

salt and freshly ground black pepper

1 Place the butter, bacon and onion in a casserole, cover and cook on full for 3 minutes.

2 Add all the remaining ingredients, stir well and heat on medium for 10–12 minutes or until piping hot. Serve with crusty bread.

Stuffed Cabbage Leaves

SERVES 4

POWER SETTINGS: FULL AND DEFROST

8 even-sized Savoy cabbage leaves, washed

2 tbsp water

FILLING

25 g/1 oz butter

1 onion, chopped

175 g/6 oz cooked chicken or veal, chopped

175 g/6 oz salami, chopped

2 tbsp chopped fresh herbs

4 slices bread, crusts removed, soaked in milk, squeezed out and crumbled

salt and freshly ground black pepper

a little olive oil

TOMATO SAUCE

2 tsp oil

½ large onion, chopped

½ clove garlic, chopped

1 small carrot, chopped

½ stick celery, chopped

1 (200-g/7-oz) can tomatoes

1½ tsp tomato purée

3–4 basil sprigs or 1 tsp dried basil

tomato wedges to garnish

1 Trim off the tough stalks at the base of the cabbage leaves. Put them in a boiling or roasting bag with the water, fasten the top loosely with a plastic tie and cook on full for 4 minutes. Lay the leaves flat on absorbent kitchen paper to drain.

2 Meanwhile make the tomato sauce, put the oil, onion, garlic, carrot and celery in a dish and cook, covered, on full for 4 minutes.

3 Stir in the tomatoes, tomato purée and basil. Cover and cook on full for 8 minutes, stirring twice.

4 Blend the sauce in a blender or food processor until smooth, then season to taste.

5 To make the filling for the cabbage leaves, put the butter and onion in a dish, cover and cook on full for 3 minutes, until soft.

6 Stir in the cooked chicken or veal, salami, herbs and bread. Season well, then divide the mixture between the cabbage leaves and roll them

up into neat parcels, folding the sides over to enclose the filling completely.

7 Pack the cabbage parcels into a dish. The dish should not be too big – the leaves must fit snugly to retain their shape during cooking. Brush the tops with a little olive oil, cover the dish and cook on defrost for 8 minutes or until hot through. Garnish with tomato wedges.

8 Heat the tomato sauce on full for about 3 minutes, then serve it with the stuffed cabbage leaves.

Stuffed Cabbage Leaves

Quick Lunch Pizzas

SERVES 4

POWER SETTING: FULL

4 thick slices wholewheat bread

1 tbsp vegetable oil

2 large tomatoes, sliced

1 tsp freshly ground black pepper

1 tsp dried basil

8 slices cheese

16 olives, stoned

1 tbsp capers

1 Toast one side of the bread under the grill, brush the untoasted side of the bread lightly with oil and arrange one layer of tomatoes on top. Sprinkle with freshly ground pepper and basil.

2 Place the sliced cheese on top, covering the centre but allowing some space for it to melt to the edge of the bread. Cover with the remaining slices of tomato.

3 Top with olives and capers and brush with oil. Arrange on a plate and microwave on full for 3 minutes. Check to see if the cheese has melted and spread, if not, cook the pizzas for a further 1 minute. The cooking time will depend on the type and thickness of the cheese used.

> COOK'S TIP
>
> *Try other toppings: for example, cooked ham, sliced mushrooms, sardines or anchovies.*

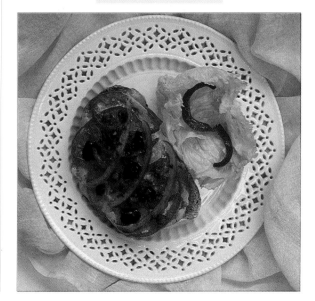

Beefburgers

SERVES 4

POWER SETTING: FULL

450 g/1 lb lean minced beef

1 onion, finely chopped

1 green pepper, seeded and chopped

2 tbsp fresh breadcrumbs

1 egg

1 tsp Worcestershire sauce

salt and freshly ground black pepper

Tomato Sauce (see page 111), to serve

GARNISH

tomato wedges

parsley sprigs

1 Place the meat in a bowl with the chopped onion and pepper. Add the breadcrumbs. Mix with a beaten egg and add the Worcestershire sauce and seasoning.

2 Divide the mixture into four portions and shape into rounds, kneading the burgers firmly into shape.

3 Heat a browning dish according to the manufacturer's instructions. Place the burgers in the dish and cook on full for 1 minute, then turn them over to brown the second side. Cook on full for a further 4 minutes, or until the burgers are cooked through. (For a really brown result, you will have to cook the first side for 2–3 minutes, then remove the burgers and reheat the dish before browning the second side.)

4 Serve the burgers coated in tomato sauce, on a bed of cooked rice or with mashed potatoes. Garnish with tomatoes and parsley. Alternatively put each burger in a toasted bun and serve with your favourite relish.

Sausage and Bacon Rolls with Tomato Rice

SERVES 4

POWER SETTING: FULL

225 g/8 oz long-grain rice

600 ml/1 pt boiling beef stock

2 tsp tomato purée

1 small onion, chopped

salt and freshly ground black pepper

8 rashers bacon, rind removed

8 sausages, grilled until brown

Tomato Sauce (see page 111), to serve

GARNISH

tomato wedges

parsley sprigs or celery leaves

1 Place the rice, beef stock, tomato purée and onion in a bowl or casserole dish. Add a pinch of salt and cover the dish. Cook on full for 15–20 minutes, or until all the liquid has been absorbed.

Beefburgers

Sausage and Bacon Rolls with Tomato Rice

2 Wrap the bacon rashers around the sausages. Place on a plate or microwave roasting rack and cover with absorbent kitchen paper. Cook on full for about 5 minutes or until the bacon is cooked.

3 Fluff up the rice with a fork, taste and season if necessary, then turn into a serving dish. Top with the sausages and spoon tomato sauce over the top.

4 Serve at once, garnished with tomato wedges and parsley sprigs or celery leaves.

COOK'S TIP

This is a good way of turning cold cooked sausages into a deliciously tasty meal.	*Instead of sausages, you can use frankfurters which do not need grilling in advance.*

Chicken Livers with Avocado

SERVES 4

POWER SETTING: FULL

25 g/1 oz butter

1 onion, sliced

675 g/1½ lb chicken livers

juice of ½ lemon

50 ml/2 fl oz dry vermouth

150 ml/¼ pt natural yogurt

salt and freshly ground black pepper

1 avocado, stoned, peeled and sliced

chopped parsley to garnish

1 Place the butter and onion in a dish and cook on full for 4 minutes. Add the chicken livers and cook, covered, on full for 2 minutes.

2 Add the lemon juice and vermouth. Stir well, cover, then cook on full for 8–10 minutes, stirring twice, until the livers are cooked.

3 Stir in the yogurt, season to taste, and cook on full for 30 seconds to warm the yogurt.

4 Spoon onto a shallow serving dish, lay the avocado slices along the livers and scatter the parsley. Serve with rice or noodles. For a richer dish use soured cream instead of the yogurt.

Sauces and Preserves

Forget about lumpy sauces and burnt sauce-pans. Go for a large basin or bowl and a whisk to make perfect sauces in the microwave. Savoury or sweet, as there is no hot base under the dish, the sauce does not stick, it is also less likely to form lumps or burn.

● Even the most delicate sauces can be prepared with ease in the microwave – for example, try the simple recipe for Hollandaise Sauce opposite.

● Although the microwave is not ideal for cooking vast quantities of preserves, it is perfect for making a few pots of jam, creamy lemon curd or a couple of pounds of chutney. Also sterilise the pots in the microwave – instructions are given in the Cook's Tip on page 116.

Béchamel Sauce

MAKES 600 ML/1 PT

POWER SETTING: FULL

600 ml/1 pt milk

¼ onion

1 bay leaf

1 bouquet garni

1 sliced carrot

40 g/1½ oz butter

50 g/2 oz plain flour

salt and freshly ground black pepper

1 Put the milk in a bowl or jug with the onion, bay leaf, bouquet garni and carrot. Cook on full for 3 minutes and allow to stand, covered, for 10 minutes. Strain.

2 Heat the butter in a bowl for 2 minutes, stir in the flour, then gradually add the milk and whisk the mixture until smooth. Season well.

3 Cook on full for 2 minutes, then whisk. Cook for a further 2 minutes, then whisk again. Cook for another 1 minute, allow to stand for 2 minutes, whisk and serve

Hollandaise Sauce

SERVES 4

POWER SETTING: FULL

175 g/6 oz butter

2 tbsp wine vinegar or lemon juice

2 egg yolks

salt and freshly ground white pepper

1 Melt the butter on full for 2 minutes. Whisk the vinegar or lemon juice with the egg yolks and seasoning.

2 Pour half the melted butter slowly onto the yolks, whisking all the time. Cook on full for 30 seconds.

3 Whisk the mixture again, then gradually pour in the remaining butter, whisking all the time. Cook for 30–60 seconds, whisk well and serve at once.

Tomato Sauce

Tomato Sauce

MAKES 600 ML/1 PT

POWER SETTING: FULL

2 tbsp oil

2 onions, chopped

1 clove garlic, crushed

1 carrot, grated

1 kg/2 lb ripe tomatoes, chopped

1 tsp sugar

1 tbsp chopped basil

1 bay leaf

1 bouquet garni

salt and freshly ground black pepper

100 ml/4 fl oz white wine or vegetable stock

1 Cook the oil, onion and garlic on full for 3 minutes. Add the carrot and cook on full for a further 2 minutes.

2 Stir in all the other ingredients, mix well and cook, covered, for 10 minutes. Allow to stand for 5 minutes. Remove the bay leaf and bouquet garni.

3 Sieve the sauce to remove the tomato skins. Reheat it on full for 2–3 minutes and serve or use as required.

Hollandaise Sauce

Hot Pepper Sauce

Hot Pepper Sauce

MAKES 600 ML/1 PT
POWER SETTING: FULL
50 ml/2 fl oz oil
10 red chillies, seeded and sliced
2 onions, chopped
1–2 cloves garlic, crushed
1 pepper, seeded and diced
1 (425-g/15-oz) can tomatoes
1 tsp salt
2 tsp mustard powder
300 ml/½ pt wine vinegar
1 bay leaf

1 Put the oil, chillies, onions and garlic in a dish, then cook for 4 minutes on full.

2 Place all the remaining ingredients in the bowl with the onion. Stir well, cover and cook on full for 10 minutes. Leave to stand for 3 minutes.

3 Cook on full for a further 10 minutes, allow to stand for 3 minutes. Then strain the sauce through a nylon sieve. Alternatively, purée it in a blender or food processor, then push through a nylon sieve to remove all skins and seeds. Pour into sterilised jars (see Microwave Tip, page 116) and cover with airtight lids. The sauce may be stored in the refrigerator for up to 2 months.

Black Cherry Sauce

SERVES 8–10
POWER SETTING: FULL
450 g/1 lb black cherries, stoned
50 g/2 oz sugar
50 ml/2 fl oz plus 1 tbsp water
1 tsp cornflour

1 Place the fruit, sugar and 50 ml/2 fl oz water in a large bowl. Cover and cook on full for about 4 minutes or until the fruit is soft. Stir halfway through cooking.

2 Blend the cornflour with the remaining 1 tbsp of water, add to the fruit and cook on full for a further minute.

Black Cherry Sauce

Summer Sauce

SERVES 8–10

POWER SETTING: FULL

225 g/8 oz red currants, washed and strung

225 g/8 oz black currants, washed and strung

225 g/8 oz raspberries, hulled

100 g/4 oz sugar

2 tbsp orange juice

2 tsp cornflour

2 tbsp water

1 Place the fruit, sugar and orange juice in a large bowl. Cover and cook on full for 4–5 minutes.

2 Combine the cornflour and water. Stir into the cooked fruit and cook, still covered, on full for 1–2 minutes, until thickened.

Summer Sauce

Chocolate Custard

MAKES 600 ML/1 PT

POWER SETTING: FULL

1 tbsp cornflour

600 ml/1 pt milk

4 egg yolks

50 g/2 oz sugar

100 g/4 oz plain chocolate, grated

1 Blend the cornflour to a smooth paste with a little of the milk. Pour the remaining milk into a microwave-proof jug and cook on full for 4–5 minutes or until very hot but not boiling. Pour the hot milk onto the cornflour mixture, return this to the jug and cook on full for a further 2–3 minutes until boiling and thickened slightly. Cool slightly, whisking well to prevent a skin forming.

2 Whisk the egg yolks and sugar together until thick and pale. Gradually pour the milk on to the eggs and sugar, whisking continuously.

3 Return the custard to the microwave and cook on full for about 2 minutes, whisking halfway through, until the custard just coats the back of a spoon. Whisk in the chocolate and serve the custard hot or cold.

4 To cool the custard, pour it into a bowl and place dampened greaseproof or waxed paper directly onto the surface to stop a skin from forming. Chill.

Chocolate Custard

From left to right: Chocolate Sauce, Fudge Sauce and Chocolate Syrup

Chocolate Sauce

SERVES 3–4

POWER SETTING: FULL

50 g/2 oz cocoa

4 tbsp golden syrup

50 g/2 oz butter

150 ml/¼ pt milk

¼ tsp vanilla essence

1 Mix the cocoa, golden syrup and butter in a small bowl. Cook on full for about 3 minutes, until melted, stir until well blended.

2 Stir in the milk and essence. Cook on full for about 2–3 minutes, until boiling. Stir well, then serve hot or cold.

VARIATIONS

Chocolate and Orange Sauce: Omit the vanilla essence but add the grated rind of ½ orange.
Honey Chocolate Sauce: Use clear honey instead of the golden syrup. Add lemon juice instead of vanilla essence.
Choco-nutty Sauce: Omit the vanilla essence. Stir in 1 tbsp smooth peanut butter.
Choco-ginger Sauce: Add 25 g/1 oz chopped stem ginger.

Chocolate Syrup

MAKES ABOUT 600 ML/1 PT

POWER SETTING: FULL

350 g/12 oz brown sugar

100 g/4 oz cocoa

300 ml/½ pt boiling water

2 tsp vanilla essence

1 In a basin, mix together the sugar and cocoa. Add the water, stirring continuously.

2 Cook on full for about 3 minutes, stirring once or twice, until the sugar dissolves. Stir in the vanilla essence, then leave to cool.

3 Serve the syrup well chilled, with ice cream, pancakes or as a flavouring for milk shakes.

Fudge Sauce

SERVES 4–6

POWER SETTING: FULL

1 tbsp cocoa

1 (175-g/6-oz) can evaporated milk

75 g/3 oz plain chocolate, grated

25 g/1 oz butter

25 g/1 oz soft brown sugar

Butterscotch Sauce

1 Put the cocoa and evaporated milk in a bowl and whisk well, then add all the remaining ingredients and whisk again.

2 Cook on full for 4–5 minutes, then whisk well to ensure that the sugar has dissolved. Serve hot or slightly warm.

Butterscotch Sauce

SERVES 4

POWER SETTINGS: FULL AND MEDIUM

100 g/4 oz soft brown sugar

50 g/2 oz butter

4 tbsp single cream

1 Place all the ingredients in a bowl and cook on full for 2 minutes.

2 Stir well, then cook on medium for a further 2 minutes. Stir well and serve.

Tobler Sauce

SERVES 4

POWER SETTING: FULL

225 g/8 oz Toblerone chocolate

150 ml/¼ pt double cream

1 Break the chocolate into pieces and place it in a basin. Cook on full for about 4 minutes, or until the chocolate has melted.

2 Stir in the cream and continue stirring until the sauce is smooth, then serve at once with ice cream or fruit.

Tobler Sauce

Fruit Chutney

MAKES 2.75 KG/6 LB

POWER SETTING: FULL

1 kg/2 lb apples, peeled, cored and sliced

1 kg/2 lb onions, sliced

grated rind and juice of 2 lemons

100 g/4 oz dried apricots, chopped

675 g/1½ lb brown sugar

600 ml/1 pt malt vinegar

1 small green chilli, seeded and chopped

225 g/8 oz sultanas

225 g/8 oz raisins

1 Place the apples and onion in a large bowl. Cover and cook for 5 minutes on full.

2 Add the lemon rind and juice, apricots and sugar. Mix well. Cook for 10 minutes on full, stirring to dissolve the sugar. When it has dissolved, add the vinegar, chilli, sultanas and raisins.

3 Cook, uncovered, for 1–1½ hours or until thick. Ladle into sterilised jars (see Microwave Tip, below), seal and label.

MICROWAVE TIP

Sterilise **metal-free** jars in the microwave: half fill them with boiling water (from the kettle) and cook on full until the water boils, then continue to cook for 3–5 minutes. Drain, dry and fill at once. If the pots are not for immediate use, cover with microwave-proof cling film for the last 1 minute of the cooking time. Leave them covered until they are used.

Lemon Curd

MAKES 675 G/1.5 LB

POWER SETTING: FULL

450 g/1 lb sugar

175 g/6 oz butter

grated rind and juice of 4 lemons

6 eggs, beaten

1 Put the sugar in a bowl. Add the butter and cook on full for 1 minute.

2 Add the rind and juice of the lemons and mix well. Strain in the beaten eggs, whisking the mixture continuously.

3 Cook on full for 2 minutes, then stir well. Cook for a further 6 minutes, stirring every 2 minutes until thickened.

4 Pot in sterilised jars, cover and store in cool place. The curd will keep for 2 weeks, or 1 month in the refrigerator.

Lemon Curd

Strawberry Jam

Three-fruit Marmalade

Three-fruit Marmalade

MAKES 2.75 KG/6 LB

POWER SETTING: FULL

450 g/1 lb oranges
1 grapefruit
2 lemons
1.75 L/3 pt boiling water
1.4 kg/3 lb sugar

1 Cook the whole fruit in two batches in the microwave oven on full for 3 minutes each.

2 Cut the fruit in half and squeeze out the juice. Slice the skins with a sharp knife or the fine slicing blade of a food processor. Put the pips in a piece of muslin or fine rinsed cloth and tie it securely.

3 Place the parcel of pips, sliced peel and water in a large bowl. Cook on full for 45 minutes.

4 Stir in the sugar until it is dissolved. If necessary, cook for 3 minutes on full power, remove and stir to dissolve the sugar.

5 When the sugar has dissolved, cook on full for 1 hour. Stir after 10 minutes, skim any foam from the surface and continue cooking.

6 Test for setting on a cold plate: if a spoonful of marmalade wrinkles after 1 minute, it has reached setting point and is ready for potting.

7 Ladle into warm sterilised jars (see Microwave Tip, left), seal and label.

VARIATION

Orange Marmalade: Use 1 kg/2 lb Seville oranges and 1 lemon. Make as above.

COOK'S TIP

This easy, cleaner way of making delicious marmalade necessitates only occasional stirring.

However, it is essential that the sugar has dissolved before boiling for a second time.

Strawberry Jam

MAKES 1.75 KG/4 LB

POWER SETTING: FULL

1 kg/2 lb strawberries, hulled
juice of 1 lemon
1 kg/2 lb sugar

1 Put the fruit in a large bowl with the lemon juice and cook for 5 minutes on full. Mash the strawberries slightly with a wooden spoon.

2 Add the sugar and stir well. Cook for 3 minutes on full and stir again. Cook on full for a further 3 minutes and stir to check the sugar has dissolved. If necessary, cook for a further 2 minutes on full.

3 Cook for another 6 minutes on full, stir thoroughly and cook for a further 6 minutes. Test for setting by putting a little jam on a cold plate; a spoonful of jam should form a skin that wrinkles after 1 minute. If not, cook for another 2 minutes on full and test again.

4 Pour or ladle into sterilised jars (see Microwave Tip, left), seal and label.

VARIATION

Raspberry Jam: Substitute raspberries for strawberries. Cook as for strawberry jam but once the sugar has dissolved, cook for a further 15 minutes on full.

Pudding and Desserts

Use the microwave to prepare stewed fruits, tempting crumbles with nutty toppings, creamy custard and light sponge puddings. In this chapter you will find plenty of ideas to suit every occasion.

- With a microwave cooker you will not be limited to turning store cupboard items like dried fruits into a delicious dessert only when you plan in advance and soak them overnight. Simply cook the fruit in liquid straight from the dried state for tender results. The method is outlined in the recipe for Hot Fruit Salad on page 123. It is also a clever dish for warming winter breakfasts as well as healthy puddings.

- Speed up the conventional cooking time of fruit pies by part-cooking the fruit in the microwave first. Allow it to cool slightly before putting in the pastry case. The results are delicious – you will be able to add lots more filling and the fruit will be deliciously soft when the pie is cut.

Christmas Pudding

MAKES 2 (600-ML/1-PT) PUDDINGS

POWER SETTING: FULL

100 g/4 oz plain flour

pinch of salt

1 tbsp mixed spice

100 g/4 oz fresh breadcrumbs

100 g/4 oz brown sugar

100 g/4 oz shredded suet

175 g/6 oz sultanas

225 g/8 oz seedless raisins

50 g/2 oz chopped mixed peel

grated rind of 1 orange

1 dessert apple, peeled, cored and grated

juice of 1 lemon

2 eggs, beaten

3 tbsp black treacle

150 ml/¼ pt stout

1 Grease two 600-ml/1-pt pudding basins. Place all the dry ingredients in a bowl and mix well. Mix the lemon juice, eggs, treacle and stout, then add this liquid to the pudding and mix thoroughly.

2 Divide the mixture between the basins pressing it down well. Cover with microwave-proof cling film and pierce the top two or three times.

3 Cook each pudding on full for 5 minutes, checking halfway through to make sure that the pudding is not overcooked. Allow to stand for 10 minutes before turning out.

MICROWAVE TIP

Christmas puddings have a very high sugar content and they do cook very quickly in the microwave. Watch them carefully as they cook.

Fruit Sponge Pudding

SERVES 6

POWER SETTING: FULL

2 tbsp jam or golden syrup

100 g/4 oz soft margarine or butter, softened

100 g/4 oz caster sugar

2 eggs

100 g/4 oz self-raising flour

50 g/2 oz glacé cherries, chopped

50 g/2 oz dried apricots, chopped

50 g/2 oz sultanas

½ tsp baking powder

2 tbsp water

1 Grease a 1-L/1¾ pt pudding basin. Place the jam or syrup in the bottom of the basin.

2 Place the margarine or butter, sugar, eggs and flour in a bowl and beat together for 1 minute. Stir in the fruit and baking powder, then stir in the water. Spoon the mixture into the basin on top of the jam. Cover with microwave-proof cling film or a greased plate (put the greased side downwards). Pierce the film two or three times. Cook on full for 6 minutes.

3 Allow to stand for 3 minutes, then turn out and serve with custard.

Snowdon Pudding

Snowdon Pudding

SERVES 4

POWER SETTING: FULL

100 g/4 oz raisins

25 g/1 oz glacé cherries, halved

100 g/4 oz shredded suet

100 g/4 oz breadcrumbs

25 g/1 oz ground rice

finely grated rind of 1 lemon

6 tbsp lemon marmalade

2 eggs, beaten

2 tbsp milk

LEMON SAUCE

4 tbsp lemon marmalade

150 ml/¼ pt hot water

1 tsp cornflour

2 tbsp cold water

1 Butter a 1.15 L/2 pt basin. Press half the raisins in the base with the glacé cherries, cut side down.

2 Place the remaining raisins, shredded suet, breadcrumbs, ground rice, lemon rind and marmalade in a mixing bowl. Mix well. Beat in the eggs and sufficient milk to make a soft dropping consistency.

3 Spoon the mixture into the basin and press it down firmly. Cover and cook on full for 9 minutes. Leave the pudding to stand for 5 minutes.

4 For the sauce, place the marmalade and hot water in a bowl and cook on full for 3 minutes. Mix the cornflour with the cold water, stir into the sauce and cook for a further 2 minutes.

5 Turn out the pudding and serve with the sauce.

Pineapple Upside-down Pudding

SERVES 4–6

POWER SETTINGS: FULL AND MEDIUM

25 g/1 oz butter

50 g/2 oz demerara sugar

1 (425-g/15-oz) can pineapple rings

6 glacé cherries

100 g/4 oz plain flour

½ tsp baking powder

100 g/4 oz margarine

100 g/4 oz caster sugar

2 eggs

1 Put the butter and demerara sugar in a 5-cm/2-in deep, 20-cm/8-in round dish and cook on full for 2 minutes until melted. Stir and make sure that the sugary syrup covers the bottom of the dish.

2 Drain the pineapple and reserve the juice. Arrange the pineapple rings and cherries in the bottom of the dish. Sift the flour and baking powder together; set aside.

3 Cream the margarine and sugar until pale and soft. Then beat in the eggs. Use a metal spoon to fold in the flour. Add a little of the reserved pineapple juice – about 2 tbsp – to soften the mixture.

4 Spread the mixture over the pineapple base and cook on medium for 10 minutes, then on full for 2 minutes, or until the sponge is just set. Allow to cool for 5 minutes in the dish, then invert the pudding onto a serving plate.

Orange Rice Pudding

Orange Rice Pudding

SERVES 2
POWER SETTINGS: FULL AND MEDIUM
50 g/2 oz pudding rice
50 g/2 oz sugar
600 ml/1 pt milk
1 tsp grated orange rind
50 g/2 oz sultanas
shredded orange rind, blanched, to decorate (optional)

1 Place all the ingredients in a 2.25-L/4-pt bowl. Cook on full for 7–8 minutes or until the milk is just boiling. Stir thoroughly.

2 Cook on medium for a further 20–25 minutes. Stir several times during cooking to prevent lumps forming.

3 Leave the pudding to stand and thicken for 7–8 minutes before serving, decorated with orange rind, if you like.

Pineapple Upside-down Pudding

Chocolate Semolina Pudding

SERVES 4

POWER SETTING: FULL

600 ml/1 pt milk

25 g/1 oz butter

2 tbsp sugar

4 tbsp semolina

50 g/2 oz plain chocolate, grated

1 Place the milk, butter and sugar in a basin and cook on full for 5 minutes.

2 Whisking continuously, slowly sprinkle in the semolina. Cook on full for 3 minutes, whisk again and cook for a further 2 minutes, or until thickened.

3 Whisk the semolina thoroughly, adding the chocolate. Whisk until the chocolate has melted and serve either hot or cold.

Apple Layer Dessert

SERVES 4

POWER SETTING: FULL

1 kg/2 lb dessert apples

2 tbsp lemon juice

75 g/3 oz ginger biscuits

50 g/2 oz soft brown sugar

50 g/2 oz sultanas

1 tsp ground cinnamon

custard or whipped cream to serve

1 Peel, core and thinly slice the apples then sprinkle with the lemon juice.

2 Crush the ginger biscuits in a polythene bag with a rolling pin. Mix the crumbs with the sugar, sultanas and ground cinnamon.

3 In a large soufflé dish, arrange alternate layers of apples and the biscuit mixture, ending with a biscuit layer on top.

4 Cook, uncovered, for 10 minutes. Serve hot or cold with custard or whipped cream.

Apple Layer Pudding

Apple and Coconut Rings

SERVES 4

POWER SETTING: FULL

6 dessert apples (about 175 g/6 oz each)

2 tbsp lemon juice

4 tbsp soft brown sugar

175 g/6 oz desiccated coconut

2 tbsp blackberry jam

1 tbsp water

glacé cherries to decorate

1 Peel and core the apples, then cut them into 5-mm/¼-in thick rings. Sprinkle with lemon juice and place on a large plate.

2 Mix the brown sugar with the coconut. Place the jam and water in a bowl and heat on full for 2 minutes, then stir well.

3 Brush the hot jam over the apple rings and cook on full for 2–3 minutes. Do not overcook the apples; they should stay firm.

4 Sprinkle the apples with the coconut mixture and transfer them to four individual serving plates. Decorate with glacé cherries and serve with whipped cream.

Hot Fruit Salad

SERVES 4

POWER SETTING: FULL

450 g/1 lb dried fruit (for example, apricots, raisins, and figs)

50 g/2 oz brown sugar

1 cinnamon stick

2 tsp lemon juice

1.15 L/2 pt boiling water

1 Place all the ingredients in a large bowl. Cover and cook on full for 15 minutes. Stir well, leave to stand for 15 minutes, then cook on full for a further 15 minutes.

2 Leave the fruit salad to stand for 30 minutes, or until soft. Cook on full for a further 5–7 minutes, until hot, before serving.

Apple Cream

SERVES 8

POWER SETTING: FULL

450 g/1 lb dessert apples, cored and sliced with their skins

juice of 1 orange

2 tbsp white wine

2 tsp orange or rose flower water

100 g/4 oz butter, softened

300 ml/½ pt double cream

1 Place the apples in a large bowl with the orange juice and wine. Cover and cook on full for 5–7 minutes, or until tender.

2 Cool slightly and purée the apples. Stir in the orange or rose flower water and beat in the butter until smooth and well blended.

3 Whip the cream until it is just beginning to thicken. Gently fold into the purée. Turn the apple cream into serving dishes and chill for at least 4 hours or until firm.

4 Serve the apple cream with plain biscuits.

Caramel Oranges

Stuffed Peaches

SERVES 4

POWER SETTING: FULL

4 peaches, stoned and halved

4 tbsp macaroon crumbs

2 tbsp finely chopped glacé cherries

8 blanched almonds

150 ml/¼ pt Marsala, Muscatel or sweet white wine

1 Remove a spoonful of flesh from each peach half but make sure you leave enough to keep the fruit firm.

2 Mash the removed flesh and mix it with the macaroon crumbs and cherries. Pile this filling into the peach halves. Top each with an almond.

3 Arrange the peaches in a shallow dish. Sprinkle with the wine, and cook on full for 4–5 minutes, until the peaches are hot through. Serve at once or allow to cool and serve chilled.

Caramel Oranges

SERVES 6

POWER SETTING: FULL

6 medium oranges

150 ml/¼ pt plus 6 tbsp water

175 g/6 oz sugar

1 Cut the rind of 2 oranges into fine shreds. Place in a basin with the 150 ml/¼ pt water and cook, covered for 5 minutes on full. Leave to stand for 15 minutes, then drain and set aside.

2 Peel away all skin and pith from the oranges. Slice them and remove the pips, then reshape them in a heatproof dish.

3 Place the sugar and remaining water in a bowl and cook on full for 2 minutes. Stir well until the sugar dissolves, then continue to cook on full for about 12 minutes, or until the syrup caramelizes. Watch the syrup carefully to make sure that it does not overcook. When the caramel is golden pour it over the oranges.

4 Cool and chill overnight. Serve the oranges decorated with the rind.

Stuffed Peaches

Chocolate Nut Slice

SERVES 8–10

POWER SETTING: FULL

175 g/6 oz plain chocolate

100 g/4 oz peanut butter

15 g/½ oz butter

2 tsp instant coffee

50 ml/2 fl oz water

100 g/4 oz icing sugar, sifted

1 egg, beaten

1 tsp vanilla essence

275 g/10 oz biscuit crumbs

150 ml/¼ pt double or whipping cream, whipped, to serve

1 Break the chocolate into a bowl. Add the peanut butter and butter and cook on full for 3–4 minutes, until the chocolate has melted and the peanut butter softened. Stir well.

2 Place the instant coffee in a mug and pour in the water, then cook on full for 30–45 seconds, or until very hot. Stir to make sure the coffee has dissolved.

3 Add the coffee and icing sugar to the chocolate mixture with the egg, vanilla essence and biscuit crumbs. Mix until the ingredients are thoroughly combined.

4 Line a 450-g/1-lb loaf tin with foil. Turn the mixture into the tin, pressing it down well and smooth the top. Freeze for at least 4 hours. To serve, cut the loaf into slices and top with piped whipped cream.

Chocolate Orange Pots

SERVES 8

POWER SETTING: FULL

175 g/6 oz plain chocolate

grated rind of 1 small orange

3 eggs, separated

2–3 tbsp orange Curaçao

250 ml/8 fl oz double cream

DECORATION

50 ml/2 fl oz double cream, lightly whipped

orange rind spirals

chocolate orange sticks

1 Put the chocolate in a bowl and melt on full for about 4 minutes. Stir halfway through and again at the end of the time.

2 Stir in the orange rind, egg yolks and liqueur. Stir well and leave to cool.

3 Whip the cream until thick. Whisk the egg whites until stiff. Fold the cream and egg whites into the chocolate mixture, and divide it between eight individual pots. Chill well.

4 Top with a little softly whipped cream and decorate with orange rind spirals and chocolate sticks.

Chocolate Fondue

SERVES 4–6

POWER SETTING: FULL

225 g/8 oz plain chocolate

225 g/8 oz milk chocolate

250 ml/8 fl oz single cream

3 tbsp Kahlua or Tia Maria

fruit, cake and biscuits to dip

1 Place the both types of chocolate together in a bowl, breaking it into small pieces, and add the cream. Cook on full for about 8–10 minutes. Stir the fondue every 2 minutes for the first 6 minutes, then every 1 minute thereafter. Cook only until all the chocolate has melted, resting for a few minutes after stirring to prevent the fondue from boiling.

2 Immediately before serving, stir in the liqueur. Place the fondue over a candle warmer for guests to dip into it.

3 Small chunks of Madeira cake or other loaf cake, marshmallows, macaroons, whole strawberries, cherries, chunks of banana and pineapple all make tasty dippers.

COOK'S TIP

To make chocolate caraque take a large slab of plain chocolate and leave it to come to room temperature, if it has been in a refrigerator. Using a kitchen knife, holding it at an acute angle to the chocolate, shave off long curls.

Pineapple Coconut Cheesecake

SERVES 8

POWER SETTING: FULL

BASE

50 g/2 oz butter

1 tbsp sugar

50 g/2 oz desiccated coconut, toasted

50 g/2 oz hazlenuts, ground

FILLING

1 (1.75-g/1-lb 13-oz) can pineapple pieces

25 g/1 oz cornflour

2 tbsp lemon juice

2 tbsp sugar

1 egg, separated

450 g/1 lb curd cheese

TOPPING

2½ tsp cornflour

1 tbsp rum

100 ml/4 fl oz water

1 Place the butter in a basin and cook on full for 1–2 minutes to melt. Stir into the other base ingredients. Press over the bottom and up the sides of a greased 20-cm/8-in loose-bottomed, deep, round flan tin.

2 For the filling, drain and reserve 100 ml/4 fl oz of the juice from the pineapple. Set aside one-third of the fruit for the top of the cheesecake. Purée the remaining fruit and juice in a blender.

3 Place the cornflour in a bowl and stir in the lemon juice, sugar and pineapple. Cook on full for 4 minutes, beating every minute, until thick.

4 Beat in the egg yolk and the curd cheese, working quickly while the mixture is very hot. Whisk the egg white until still, then fold it into the cheesecake mixture. Turn the mixture into the tin and leave to cool. Chill for at least 4 hours or overnight.

5 For the topping, blend the cornflour with the reserved juice, rum and water. Cook on full for about 4 minutes, until boiling and thickened. Whisk well and leave to cool slightly.

6 Top the cheesecake with the reserved fruit and glaze with the cooled sauce. Remove from the tin when set and serve with whipped cream.

Pineapple Coconut Cheesecake

Chocolate and Coffee Bavarois

SERVES 6–8

POWER SETTING: FULL

4 egg yolks

50 g/2 oz sugar

1 tsp vanilla essence

600 ml/1 pt milk

175 g/6 oz plain chocolate, grated

1 tbsp coffee essence

4 tbsp cold water

15 g/½ oz powdered gelatine

150 ml/¼ pt double cream

150 ml/¼ pt single cream

2 egg whites

DECORATION

150 ml/¼ pt double cream, whipped

chocolate caraque (see Cook's Tip, left)

1 In a bowl beat together the egg yolks, sugar and vanilla essence until pale and creamy.

2 Place the milk in a microwave-proof jug and heat for 4–5 minutes until hot but not boiling. Stir into the egg yolk mixture and cook on full for 5–7 minutes, stirring every minute. The cooked custard should be slightly thickened. Watch it as it cooks and do not allow it to boil or it will curdle.

3 Add the chocolate and coffee essence to the custard. Stir until completely dissolved.

4 Put the water in a small basin and heat on full for 30 seconds. Sprinkle in the gelatine, leave to soften for 2 minutes, then stir until the gelatine has dissolved completely.

5 Stir the gelatine into the chocolate custard. Leave until the mixture begins to thicken. Whip the creams together until thick. Whisk the egg whites until stiff.

6 Fold the cream into the chocolate mixture, then fold the egg whites into the mixture. Pour into a lightly-oiled, 1.4-L/2½-pt mould. Chill until set.

7 Turn the Bavarois out onto a serving plate. Decorate with piped whipped cream and chocolate caraque.

Bread, Cakes and Biscuits

The microwave will not cook a cake in the same way as the conventional oven but it is useful for making a cake or a few rolls of bread when you are in a hurry.

● It is also a good way of introducing the children to cooking – help them to make some biscuits and cook them in the microwave instead of risking burns on a hot conventional oven.

● The microwave can be used for defrosting frozen breads and cakes. The following chart offers a guide to timings.

Cakes, Bread and Desserts Defrosting Guide

FOOD	QUANTITY	MINUTES ON LOW	STANDING MINUTES
bread, whole loaf	1 large	6–8	5–15
bread, whole loaf	1 small	4–6	10
bread, sliced loaf	1 large	6–8	10
bread, sliced loaf	1 small	4–6	5
bread slice	25 g/1 oz	10–15 seconds	1–2
bread rolls, crumpets, scones etc.	2 4	15–20 seconds 25–35 seconds	1–2 1–2
cakes, cream	2 4	45–60 seconds 1	10 10
cakes, small cupcakes	2 4	30–60 seconds ¼–1¾	5 5
cakes, large sponge cake	450 g/1 lb	4	10
cheesecake	23 cm/9 in	3–4	20
dough, pizza and bread	450 g/1 lb	4	10
mousse, individual	1	30 seconds	15
pastry, shortcrust and puff	225g g/8 oz 397 g/14 oz	4 6	20 20
pie, fruit	650 g/26 oz	5	10
trifle, individual	1	1	15

White Bread

MAKES A (1-KG/2-LB) LOAF

POWER SETTING: FULL

1 tsp sugar

300 ml/½ pt warm water

1 tsp dried yeast

450 g/1 lb strong plain flour

½ tsp salt

40 g/½ oz butter

2 tsp oil

1 tbsp poppy seeds

1 Grease a 1-kg/2-lb loaf dish or a large soufflé dish, and line the bottom with greaseproof or waxed paper.

2 Place the sugar in a jug with half the water. Cook on full for 30 seconds. Stir in the yeast and allow to stand for 10–15 minutes, or until frothy.

3 Sift the flour and salt into a bowl and cook on full for 30 seconds, then rub in the butter. Make a well in the middle, then pour in the yeast liquid and the remaining water. Gradually work the dry ingredients into the liquid to make a firm dough. Knead thoroughly on a lightly floured surface until the dough is smooth and elastic.

4 Place the dough in a floured bowl and cover with microwave-proof cling film. Cook on full for 15 seconds to prove. Leave to stand in a warm place until the dough has risen to double its original size.

5 Turn the dough onto a floured surface, knead for a further 2–3 minutes. Place in the dish, then cover with a clean damp tea towel and leave in a warm place until doubled in size.

6 Oil the top of the loaf and sprinkle with the poppy seeds. Cook on full for 5 minutes, turning once. Allow to stand for 10 minutes. Turn out onto a cooling rack and allow to cool completely. Brown the crust under the grill, if liked.

Wholewheat Rolls

Jam and Cream Sandwich Cake

SERVES ABOUT 8
POWER SETTING: FULL
175 g/6 oz butter
175 g/6 oz caster sugar
3 eggs, beaten
175 g/6 oz plain flour
¾ tsp baking powder
pinch of salt
about 2 tbsp warm milk
5 tbsp strawberry jam
150 ml/¼ pt whipping cream, whipped
icing sugar to dust

1 Line a 20-cm/8-in round, straight-sided, deep dish with microwave-proof cling film.

2 Cream the butter with the sugar until soft and light. Gradually beat in the eggs. Sift the flour with the baking powder and salt. Use a metal spoon to fold it into the creamed mixture a third

at a time, adding enough milk to make the mixture drop easily from the spoon.

3 Spoon the mixture into the dish and cook on full for 6–8 minutes. When cooked, the cake should still look slightly moist on top, but this will dry out. Allow to stand for 5 minutes before turning out and cooling completely on a wire rack.

4 When cool, remove the cling film and carefully slice the cake in half horizontally. Spread the base with jam and whipped cream, then top with the second half. Dredge with icing sugar.

Wholewheat Rolls

MAKES 16
POWER SETTING: FULL
300 ml/½ pt milk
2 tsp dried yeast
1 tsp caster sugar
450 g/1 lb wholewheat flour
1 tsp salt
2 tsp malt extract
2 tbsp oil
1 egg, beaten
2 tsp poppy seeds

1 Pour the milk into a jug and cook on full for 30 seconds. Stir in the yeast and sugar. Allow to stand for 15 minutes, or until frothy.

Jam and Cream Sandwich Cake

2 Place the flour and salt in a large bowl and cook on full for 30 seconds.

3 Make a well in the middle of the dry ingredients, then pour in the yeast liquid, malt extract and oil. Work the flour into the liquid to make a firm dough. Turn the dough out onto a floured surface and knead thoroughly until smooth and elastic. Place in a floured bowl, cover with microwave-proof cling film and cook on full for 15 seconds to prove. Leave to stand in a warm place until the dough has risen to double its original size.

4 Knead lightly, divide into sixteen portions and shape into rolls. Place the rolls in two large, floured flan dishes. Cover with a damp tea towel and leave in a warm place to rise for a further 20 minutes, or until doubled in size.

5 Brush with beaten egg and sprinkle with poppy seeds. Bake in two batches on full for 3–4 minutes each.

6 Allow to cool on a wire rack. For a crisper, browner crust, brown the cooked rolls under the grill.

Gingerbread

SERVES 6–10

POWER SETTING: FULL

8 tbsp black treacle
75 g/3 oz brown sugar
100 g/4 oz butter or margarine
100 g/4 oz self-raising flour
100 g/4 oz wholewheat flour
½ tsp bicarbonate of soda
1 tsp ground ginger
1 tsp ground mixed spice
2 eggs, beaten

1 Place the treacle, sugar and butter or margarine in a bowl and cook on full for 2 minutes. Allow to stand for 2 minutes.

2 Stir in the flours, bicarbonate of soda and spices, then beat in the eggs.

3 Grease a 1-kg/2-lb loaf dish or a deep oblong dish and pour in the mixture. Cook on full for 4 minutes, turning twice.

4 Allow to stand for 5 minutes before turning out onto a wire rack to cool completely. Serve cut into slices and buttered.

Gingerbread

Orange Sponge Cake

SERVES 10

POWER SETTING: FULL

225 g/8 oz plain flour

1 tsp baking powder

100 g/4 oz butter

100 g/4 oz brown sugar

2 eggs

2 tbsp orange juice

grated rind of half an orange

50 g/2 oz candied orange peel, chopped

DECORATION

225 g/8 oz icing sugar

2 tbsp water

orange food colouring

jellied orange slices

1 Sift the flour and baking powder into a mixing bowl. Rub in the butter until the mixture resembles fine breadcrumbs. Add the sugar, then make a well in the mixture and break in the eggs. Gradually beat the eggs into the mixture. Stir in orange juice, orange rind and candied peel.

2 Line and grease an 18-cm/7-in round straight-sided deep dish.

3 Spoon the sponge mixture into the prepared dish and cook on full for 5 minutes. Allow the cake to stand in the dish for 5 minutes before turning out onto a wire rack to cool completely.

4 Mix the icing sugar with the water and a few drops of orange food colouring. Coat the cake with icing and decorate with jellied orange slices.

Carrot Cake

MAKES 1 (20-CM/8-IN) CAKE

POWER SETTING: FULL

100 g/4 oz carrots, grated

2 tbsp orange juice

50 g/2 oz butter

100 g/4 oz brown sugar

2 eggs

175 g/6 oz self-raising flour

1/4 tsp ground cinnamon

50 g/2 oz walnuts, chopped

CREAM CHEESE FROSTING

25 g/1 oz unsalted butter

75 g/3 oz icing sugar

grated rind of 1 lemon

225 g/8 oz cream cheese

coarsely grated lemon or orange rind to decorate

1 Line a 20-cm/8-in round, deep dish with microwave-proof cling film. Place the carrots and orange juice in a basin. Cover and cook on full for 10 minutes, stirring halfway through cooking. Leave until cold.

2 Cream the butter and sugar together. Beat in the eggs, one at a time. Sift the flour, and cinnamon, and stir into the creamed mixture.

3 Fold in the carrots and nuts. Turn into the prepared dish, smooth the top and cook on full for 6–8 minutes, until the cake is risen but still slightly moist on top. Leave to stand for 10 minutes, then cool on a rack.

4 When the cake is cold remove the film. Beat all the ingredients for the frosting together or process them in a food processor. Spread over the cake and decorate with the rind.

Family Chocolate Cake

MAKES 1 (20-CM/8-IN) CAKE

POWER SETTING: FULL

75 g/3 oz plain chocolate

2 tbsp clear honey

100 g/4 oz butter or margarine

75 g/3 oz sugar

2 eggs

150 g/5 oz self-raising flour

25 g/1 oz cocoa

¼ tsp vanilla essence

150 ml/¼ pt milk

ICING

50 g/2 oz plain chocolate

3 tbsp water

25 g/1 oz butter

200 g/7 oz icing sugar, sifted

1 Line a 20-cm/8-in round, deep cake dish or soufflé dish with microwave-proof cling film. Put the chocolate and the honey into a small bowl and cook on full for about 2–3 minutes, or until melted.

2 Cream the butter or margarine and sugar together until light and fluffy, then beat in the chocolate mixture and the eggs.

3 Sift the flour and cocoa and stir into the creamed mixture with the vanilla essence and milk.

4 Pour the mixture into the prepared dish and cook on full for 6–8 minutes, or until risen but still slightly moist on top. Leave to stand in the dish for 5 minutes.

5 Turn on to a wire rack and remove the film. Leave to cool.

6 To make the icing, put the chocolate and water into a small basin and cook on full for 1–2 minutes or until melted. Stir in the butter, cooking for a further 30 seconds if necessary. When the butter has melted, beat in the icing sugar. Set the icing aside until firm enough to swirl on top of the cake.

7 Spread the icing over the top of the cake and swirl it with a palette knife.

Black Forest Cake

MAKES 1 (20-CM/8-IN) CAKE

POWER SETTING: FULL

175 g/6 oz self-raising flour

50 g/2 oz cocoa

100 g/4 oz brown sugar

100 g/4 oz molasses

100 g/4 oz butter, softened

2 eggs, beaten

1 tsp vanilla essence

150 ml/¼ pt single cream

FILLING AND DECORATION

about 450 g/1 lb canned black cherries (or fresh fruit)

75 ml/2½ fl oz cherry juice

100 ml/4 fl oz kirsch

600 ml/1 pt double cream, whipped

grated chocolate

red currant jelly, warmed

chocolate caraque (see Cook's Tip, page 126)

icing sugar

1 Line a 20-cm/8-in round, deep dish with microwave-proof cling film.

2 Sift the flour and cocoa into a bowl and stir in the sugar. Make a well in the middle and add the molasses, butter and eggs. Beat the ingredients, gradually working in the flour and adding the vanilla essence and cream.

3 Turn the mixture into the prepared dish and cook on full for 6 minutes, or until the cake has risen but is still slightly moist on top. Leave in the dish for 10 minutes, then cool on a wire rack and remove the film.

4 Reserve some of the cherries for decoration. Split the cake into four layers. Mix together the juice and kirsch. Sprinkle a little over one cake layer. Spread with a little cream and top with a few cherries.

5 Lay the second cake layer on top and repeat the layering process. Repeat with the third layer. Top with the last cake layer and spread the surface and sides with the remaining whipped cream.

6 Press grated chocolate firmly over the sides with a palette knife. Pipe two rows of cream around the top edge of the cake. Place the reserved cherries between the rows of cream. Brush the cherries lightly with a little warmed red currant jelly.

7 Pile chocolate caraque in the centre of the cake. Sprinkle lightly with icing sugar.

Flapjacks

MAKES 12 FLAPJACKS

POWER SETTING: FULL

75 g/3 oz butter

3 tbsp golden syrup

100 g/4 oz porridge oats

25 g/1 oz brown sugar

25 g/1 oz chopped mixed peel

1 Line a shallow 20 × 25-cm/8 × 10-in dish with microwave-proof cling film.

2 Place the butter and syrup in a bowl and cook on full for 1 minute. Stir in the oats, sugar and peel, mixing thoroughly, then press the mixture into the dish and mark into twelve pieces.

3 Cook on full for 3 minutes. Cool slightly, then cut the pieces and allow to cool completely on a wire rack.

Refrigerator Biscuit Cake

MAKES 1 (450-G/1-LB) CAKE

POWER SETTING: FULL

225 g/8 oz milk chocolate

100 g/4 oz butter

50 g/2 oz golden syrup

50 g/2 oz raisins, soaked overnight in a little rum

50 g/2 oz brazil nuts, roughly chopped

50 g/2 oz glacé cherries, roughly chopped

225 g/8 oz digestive biscuits, crushed

DECORATION

glacé cherries

whole brazil nuts

1 Line a 450-g/1-lb loaf tin with greaseproof paper and lightly oil it. Put the chocolate, butter and golden syrup in a basin and cook on full for 4–6 minutes or until the chocolate has melted. Stir in the raisins, nuts and cherries.

2 Add the biscuits and mix well together. Press the mixture into the prepared tin and chill for at least 4 hours, preferably overnight.

3 Turn out and decorate with glacé cherries and brazil nuts, then cut into slices and serve.

Brownies

MAKES ABOUT 10

POWER SETTING: FULL

100 g/4 oz butter, melted

100 g/4 oz soft brown sugar

25 g/1 oz cocoa, sifted

50 g/2 oz self-raising flour, sifted

1 egg

1 tbsp milk

25 g/1 oz walnuts, finely chopped

25 g/1 oz raisins, chopped

ICING

100 g/4 oz plain chocolate

1 tbsp black coffee

walnut halves to decorate

1 Place the butter in a basin and melt on full for about 1–1½ minutes.

2 Mix together the sugar, cocoa and flour. Beat together the egg and milk. Stir into the flour mixture, together with the butter, walnuts and raisins.

3 Spread in a greased and base-lined shallow dish measuring 18 × 28 cm/7 × 11 in. Cook on full for 2–3 minutes, then leave to cool in the dish.

4 For the icing, place the chocolate and coffee in a basin and cook on full for 3–4 minutes.

5 Spread the icing over the cake. When almost set cut the brownies into squares and top each portion with a piece of walnut.

Chocolate Meringues

MAKES 15–20
POWER SETTING: FULL
1 large egg white
275 g/10 oz icing sugar, sifted
15 g/½ oz cocoa, sifted
FILLING
150 ml/¼ pt double cream
1 tbsp soft brown sugar
2 tsp cocoa

1 Break up the egg white with a fork, then gradually work in the icing sugar and cocoa to make a firm, smooth fondant.

2 Break off small portions of fondant, about the size of a walnut. Roll them into balls and cook six at a time.

3 Place the six chocolate meringues on a large flan dish or flat plate lined with non-stick cooking parchment. Arrange the meringues in a circle, as far apart as possible.

4 Cook on full for about 1 minute, until the meringues stay puffed. Cool on a wire rack. Cook the remaining mixture.

5 Whip the cream until stiff. Stir in the sugar and cocoa. Sandwich the meringues together, two at a time, with the chocolate cream.

Chocolate Chip Cookies

MAKES 12
POWER SETTING: FULL
50 g/2 oz brown sugar
50 g/2 oz butter or margarine
½ tsp vanilla essence
2 tbsp chopped walnuts
75 g/3 oz self-raising flour
15 g/½ oz cocoa
25 g/1 oz chocolate drops for cooking
1 tbsp water

1 Cream the sugar, butter or margarine and vanilla essence until very soft.

2 Stir in the remaining ingredients, adding the water if necessary to make a stiff mixture.

3 Shape into twelve small balls about the size of walnuts and place them as far apart as possible round the edge of a flat, shallow dish.

4 Flatten the cookies, then cook on full for 2 minutes or until the cookies are firm. Leave on the dish for 4–5 minutes, then lift them onto a wire rack to cool.

Sweet Treats

For Christmas or birthdays, or just when you feel like a treat, make a little tray of goodies in the microwave. Here you will find a selection of recipes for chocolate-based sweets and for favourite Coconut Ice or very quick Chocolate Crispies.

● Even if you are not preparing treats, the microwave is very useful for melting chocolate for icings or sauces. Simply place cubes of chocolate in a basin and cook on full for the suggested time. The squares of chocolate may not look melted but when you give them a stir you will find that they are quite soft.

● To make a real cheat's treat, simply melt bought toffees with some chocolate, then stir in chopped nuts, cherries and raisins. Divide the mixture between sweet cases or leave to set in a tray, then cut it into cubes. Everyone will be impressed with your attempts if you forget to admit that you bought the toffee!

Chocolate Crispies

MAKES 24

POWER SETTING: FULL

175 g/6 oz butter

175 g/6 oz plain or milk chocolate

175 ml/6 fl oz golden syrup

175 g/6 oz cornflakes or Rice Crispies

1 Melt the butter, chocolate and syrup together in a bowl on full for about 5–6 minutes, stir well.

2 Add the cornflakes or Rice Crispies and mix thoroughly.

3 Place 24 paper cups on a tray and spoon the cereal mixture into these cases. Leave to set for at least 8 hours.

VARIATION

Press the cereal mixture into the paper cups making a hollow space in the centre which can be filled with fruit and cream before serving.

Coconut Ice

MAKES 450 G/1 LB

POWER SETTING: FULL

450 g/1 lb sugar

150 ml/¼ pt milk

100 g/4 oz desiccated coconut

1 tbsp double cream

few drops of red food colouring

1 Butter a 20-cm/8-in square tin. Stir the sugar and milk in a large bowl until the sugar has dissolved. Cook on full for 6–8 minutes. The mixture should reach the soft ball stage: to test, drop a little of the mixture in cold water, it should form a soft ball when rolled between the fingers. Check for this stage after 5 minutes and then every minute until ready. Stir occasionally.

2 Stir in the coconut and cream, then beat well until the mixture is thick and creamy. Pour half the mixture into the prepared tin.

3 Colour the remaining mixture pink and spread it over the white layer. Cool until firm and set. Mark into squares and cut into pieces when cold.

Rich Chocolate Truffles

MAKES ABOUT 30

POWER SETTING: FULL

225 g/8 oz plain or milk chocolate

100 g/4 oz butter

2 tsp liqueur (for example Tia Maria, Contreau, rum or brandy)

175 g/6 oz icing sugar

ground nuts or chocolate vermicelli to coat

1 Place the chocolate in a bowl and cook on full for about 8 minutes, or until melted. Stir the chocolate every 2 minutes to prevent it overcooking at the edges.

2 Add the butter and liqueur and beat until smooth. Beat in the icing sugar, then chill well until firm.

3 Shape into 2.5-cm/1-in balls and roll in the nuts or chocolate vermicelli. Place the truffles in paper cases and keep them cool.

VARIATIONS

The truffles can be coated in icing sugar, cocoa powder, drinking chocolate powder, ground praline or grated chocolate.

Cherry Chocolate Crunch

SERVES 8–10

POWER SETTING: FULL

100 g/4 oz plain chocolate

100 g/4 oz butter

1 egg

100 g/4 oz digestive biscuits, crushed

50 g/2 oz glacé cherries, chopped

50 ml/2 fl oz rum

2 tbsp chopped nuts

1 Melt the chocolate with the butter in a bowl on full for 5–6 minutes. Stir well.

2 Lightly beat the egg and stir into the melted chocolate. Add all the remaining ingredients and mix well so that the biscuit crumbs are well coated with chocolate.

3 Turn the mixture into a well-greased 20-cm/8-in round, shallow, cake tin. Chill for at least 8 hours before serving, cut into wedges.

Chocolate-dipped Fruit

Chocolate-dipped fruits

SERVES 8

POWER SETTING: FULL

450 g/1 lb fresh fruit (for example strawberries, grapes, cherries, mandarin segments and peeled lychees)

450 g/1 lb plain chocolate

1 Make sure the fruit is firm. Wash and dry well, leaving stalks on where applicable.

2 Break the chocolate into a bowl and cook on full for 3 minutes. Stir well, cook for a further 3 minutes and stir again. Cook on full for a further 2–3 minutes, or until the chocolate has melted.

3 Holding a piece of fruit by the stem, or using a cocktail stick to skewer it, dip half-way into the chocolate. Leave the top half uncovered. Shake off the excess chocolate.

4 Place the fruit on a tray lined with non-stick or waxed paper and leave in a cool place to dry.

5 The dipped fruits can be served as they are or in petit fours cases. Serve on the same day as they are prepared.

VARIATIONS

Crystallized orange peel, crystallized ginger, and pineapple may also be dipped in this way. These will also keep longer, so are better for present giving.

Chocolate Peppermint Creams

Chocolate Peppermint Creams

MAKES ABOUT 40

POWER SETTING: FULL

1 large egg white

1/4 tsp peppermint essence

a few drops green or pink food colouring (optional)

350 g/12 oz icing sugar, sifted

a little cornflour

100 g/4 oz plain or milk chocolate

1 Put the egg white, essence and colouring in a bowl. Gradually stir in the icing sugar until a stiff paste is formed. Knead until smooth.

2 Lightly dust a board with cornflour. Roll out the paste to about 5 mm/¼ in thick. Using 4-cm/1½-in fancy cutters (fluted, hearts and diamonds, for example) cut out shapes and place them on non-stick paper. Leave to dry overnight.

3 Break the chocolate into a basin and cook on full for about 4–5 minutes, stirring frequently until it has melted. Stir until smooth.

4 Dip each sweet in the chocolate so only half is coated. Shake off any drips. Place on non-stick or waxed paper and leave to set.

Chocolate Fudge

MAKES ABOUT 675 G/1½ LB
POWER SETTING: FULL
450 g/1 lb icing sugar, sifted
4 tbsp milk
100 g/4 oz butter, cut into pieces
175 g/6 oz chocolate, broken into squares
50 g/2 oz set honey

1 Put the icing sugar in a large bowl and make a well in the middle. Place the milk, butter, chocolate and honey in the well and cook on full for about 4 minutes, or until the chocolate and butter are melted.

2 Gradually stir the icing sugar into the melted ingredients, then beat the mixture thoroughly

Chocolate Fudge

until smooth. Pour the fudge into an oiled 20-cm/8-in square tin and chill until set.

3 Cut the fudge into 2.5-cm/1-in squares. It can be stored in an airtight container in the refrigerator, placing sheets of waxed paper between the layers.

Toffee Apple Treat

Toffee Apple Treat

SERVES 4
POWER SETTING: FULL
4 dessert apples
450 g/1 lb treacle toffee
1 tbsp water
50 g/2 oz chopped nuts

1 Peel and core the apples, then cut each into eight pieces.

2 Place the toffee and water in a bowl and cook on full for 3–4 minutes or until the toffee has melted. Stir after 2 minutes.

3 Spear the apple pieces on wooden cocktail sticks, dip them in the toffee and sprinkle with the chopped nuts. Stand them on greased greaseproof paper and chill for 1 hour.

Index